What I Learned at Bug Camp

What I Learned at Bug Camp
Essays on Finding a Home in the World

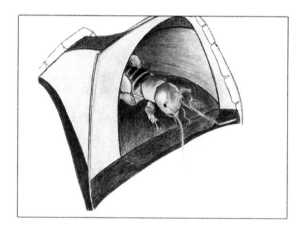

Sarah Juniper Rabkin

WITH ILLUSTRATIONS BY THE AUTHOR

Grateful acknowledgment is made to the original publishers for permission to reprint the following essays:

"Eyes of the World," originally published in *The Way of Natural History*, ed. Thomas Lowe Fleischner (San Antonio, TX: Trinity University Press, 2011).

"A Back Road Home," an earlier version of which was originally published as "Saltshakers and Parachutes" in *Storming Heaven's Gate: An Anthology of Spiritual Writings by Women*, ed. Amber Coverdale Sumrall and Patrice Vecchione (New York: Plume, 1997), 37–49.

"A Great Excuse to Stare," an earlier version of which was originally published in *The Alphabet of the Trees: A Guide to Nature Writing*, ed. Christian McEwen and Mark Statman (New York: Teachers & Writers Collaborative, 2000), 87–92.

Earlier versions of the following essays originally appeared elsewhere:

"What I Learned at Bug Camp" in *ISLE (Interdisciplinary Studies in Literature and Environment)* 11, no. 2 (2004) 195–210.

"An Incredibly Stupid Flirtation with Death," as "In Flirting with Death, a Vivid Taste of Life," in the *Los Angeles Times* Outdoors section, September 13, 2005.

"Why Dolphins Help," as "Why Do Dolphins Help," in *Whalewatcher* 19, no. 4 (1985).

"Confluence" in *The Lavender Reader*, Summer 1991.

"Coming around the Bend" in *Places: A Quarterly Journal of Environmental Design* 8, no. 4 (1993).

"Musical Medicine" in the *Santa Cruz Sun*, June 25, 1987.

"Cupid's Chemistry" in the *Santa Cruz Sun*, October 9, 1986.

"Lessons from the Sharp End of the Pen" in *Faculty Focus: A Quarterly Newsletter from the University of California, Santa Cruz, Center for Teaching Excellence* 12, no. 1 (2006).

"Sailing into Now," as "Setting Sail for the Present," in *Writing Nature*, Summer 1999.

"Cultural Cosmetics / Cosmetic Culture," as "Breaking the Mold," in the *Santa Cruz Sun*, September 11, 1986.

What I Learned at Bug Camp: Essays on Finding a Home in the World.

Copyright © 2011 by Sarah Rabkin.

Juniper Lake Press
P.O. Box 7467
Santa Cruz, CA 95061
http://www.juniperlakepress.com

ISBN: 978-0-9843196-1-9   Cover design by Sandy Bell.

For Chuck

TABLE OF CONTENTS

LIVING TOGETHER

INTRODUCTION

Notes from the Trail

I like hiking alone, but a fear of creek crossings holds me back. I have no problem walking over wide, well-built bridges. I can even deal with a handmade wooden span or a swinging rope walkway, as long as there's a sturdy guardrail. But when the path leads to a riverbank beyond which lies nothing more substantial than a slippery log, a hammock of tangled branches, or a series of widely spaced rocks, I balk.

I'm apt to wander a considerable distance up and down the bank, seeking an easier way across. If the waterway is shallow and tame, I'll trade my boots for sandals, fording the current with feet planted on cobble, silt, or sand. But on more than one occasion, I've aborted a solo hike through beautiful country—just turned around and walked back to the trailhead—simply because I couldn't bring myself to cross a stream.

My body is partly to blame. It's gained a few pounds and shed some balance and grace. This makes me unstable with a pack on my back. Also, at four feet eleven inches tall, I am forced to leap between creek boulders that, for others, are spaced an easy step apart. The real problem, though, is my mind. Gazing at a felled tree trunk stretching from bank to bank, I envision all the ways I might lose my footing, flail helplessly, and pitch off the log into the torrent below, with nobody around to help. Hiking companions can reassure or embarrass me across; alone, I play it safe and give up the adventure.

I hate curtailing my explorations out of fear, and so, in recent years, I have been trying to curtail the fear itself. A mantra helps. I received my first one from a fellow hiker on a Yosemite backpacking trip. A shy, nineteen-year-old Chicano, he rarely spoke with any of the dozen other people on the week-long walk. But one morning, he waited patiently behind me as I picked my way across a rock-strewn stream. Eventually, he said to my back—quietly and without rancor—"You think too much. Just do it." And I did. I decided to trust that if I could just keep moving, my feet would land in the right places. Before long, I had reached the far bank.

On a later outing, I discovered that I could keep the fear in check by concentrating on the narrow platform beneath my feet. I tried to follow the credo of Yosemite's climber-philosopher Ron Kauk: "Let go of everything but what you need to stay on the rock." Shutting out all awareness of fast water or precipitous heights, refusing to entertain visions of calamity, I told myself, "Right now, there's nothing in the universe but this safe, solid log."

This has become a rhythmic refrain that hums through my mind during any crossing: "Nothing but the log; nothing but the log; *nothingbutthelog*." Mumbling it to myself has gotten me across many a creek—not by vanquishing fear but by displacing it with single-minded momentum. Now, when I hear the rush of mountain water up ahead or come around a bend to behold a rickety construction spanning a gulch, the familiar adrenaline spike may be accompanied by a feisty inner voice: "Let's go, my friend. You can *do* this."

To compose a personal essay, I find, requires a kind of metaphorical creek crossing. What usually motivates me to start writing is the desire to move through some new stretch of emotional, intellectual, ethical country: to discover the inhabitants of this landscape, feel its breezes, take in the view from its heights. The beckoning terrain may open up out of an unfinished conversation that I can't get out of my head. The topography may feature a preoccupying passion, a confounding question, a patch of despair. If it's country worth exploring in an essay and if I'm writing honestly, then eventually the trail winds up at the lip of a gorge—and then another and another. These are junctures where I'm forced to face the limits of my understanding, to explore beyond habitual platitudes and into the unknown.

Though I may search upstream and down for an easier route, it usually becomes apparent that the only way beyond is directly across. As Arthur Miller observed, "The writer must be in it; he can't be to one side of it, ever. He has to be endangered by it. His own attitudes have to be tested in it. The best work that anybody ever writes is on the verge of embarrassing him, always."

And so I spend a fair amount of my writing time staring across one abyss or another, eyeing the meager bridges on offer. To test my own attitudes repeatedly and find a way to new ground is for me the most rewarding aspect of essay writing. Not only does the process continually extend my limited horizons; if I manage to tell a good story with sufficient integrity, the resulting piece of prose may also help a reader negotiate a dicey crossing of her own.

That's the aim. But bridging from one stretch of territory to the next can be daunting, even frightening. When I sit at the laptop wrestling with some challenging argument, my pulse may quicken as at a rain-slicked log bridge. The anxiety is similar. Weighed down by a pack of jumbled thoughts, I become preoccupied with the ineptitude revealed by my halting steps. Worse, I imagine myself crashing into the drop, where specious conclusions rear up and rough currents threaten. I want to make it to the other side, where I can already catch glimpses of clarity and insight, but I'm not sure I have what it takes.

At such times, I call on the writer's equivalent of a "nothing but-the-log" mantra. I have to keep returning my attention to questions and images that seem alive, unpredictable, hot to the touch. I try to lay a hand on the vital pulse that thrums through those passages; I do my best to resist the glib formulations that have a way of crowding in. Finding the truest route entails an unpredictable foray through research and reason, imagination and craft.

It's a slow process, at least for this author. The pieces in this collection have accrued over the course of many years, during which essay writing has become a steadying and sustaining practice. All of the book's contents, whether they focus on field entomology or erotic desire, cosmetic surgery or the lives of dolphins, reflect this seeker's quest for a sense of home in a complicated world.

While this journey is essentially solitary, there are moments when a helping hand can ease the crossing. Friends, teachers, and colleagues—a *lot* of them, as the acknowledgments attest—have handed me hiking poles along the way. Their insights and encouragement make my work far more effective than if I'd traveled alone.

My Outward-Bound-for-essayists approach has helped me explore an eclectic assortment of topics—light and weighty, introspective and reportorial, rooted in the arts or in the sciences or (most often) somewhere in between. But the ideas that preoccupy me do cluster into a few rough categories, and three of these make up the book's section headings. "Creature Comforts" comprises essays that explore the workings of the natural world, both within and beyond these bodies we call human. As individuals and as a race, our fates are so utterly entwined with realities inside and outside our own skin that I cannot begin to make sense of my experience without exploring those interdependencies. "Drawing

Lessons" ambles around the educational landscape, high-lighting insights I've gleaned as both a teacher and a student. And "Living Together" offers some musings about community: how it fails and how it can thrive.

If you come with me on these rambles, I'll show you a view from the far side of the creek.

CREATURE COMFORTS

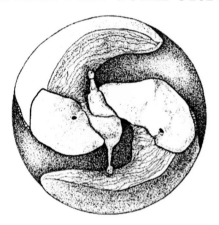

What I Learned at Bug Camp

All the sciences and arts are taught as if they were separate. They are separate only in the classroom. Step out . . . and they are immediately fused.
—Aldo Leopold

Deep in the heart of the castle that she and her king founded long ago, an enormous queen reclines on a platform from which she has not moved in years. Armed guards patrol the entrances to her temperature-controlled chamber. The translucent body that extends behind the queen's dark head is disproportionately large, like a school bus grafted to a VW. Nonstop convulsions ripple down its length. From the nether end of this pulsing tube emerge eggs like fat rice rains, thirty thousand of them a day, spirited away by small blind attendants as quickly as the queen can pump them out.

"*Gross!*" protests a sixteen-year-old girl, raising her voice above the sprocket-song of the projector. It's 1981. Fresh out of college, I have parlayed a bare-bones biology BA into a job teaching high school science. I have shown this documentary film about African termite colonies to every one of my biology classes, and although most of my students seem less than enthralled, I cannot get enough.

As a child grubbing in my back yard in Northern California, I once unearthed an especially beefy insect—two inches long, shiny and wingless, with beady dark eyes in a huge, blank, amber head. It had spiny legs and an ample body ringed with convict stripes. I recoiled. Yet for days afterward, I couldn't stop thinking about that creature. How did it spend its days and nights, out there under the rocks and dirt? What did it eat? Why did it need those scary spines?

Even now, many years later, curiosity still edges out my visceral shiver at such encounters. I left formal science study behind after college, but questions about insects kept buzzing in my head. One winter afternoon, as I passed a bulletin board at the university where I work, a flyer caught my eye. Decorated with line drawings of ants, aphids, and wasps, it advertised a summer field course in entomology:

> *Insect diversity and natural history in the California Sierra Nevada. An intensive five-week course with excursions to different habitats ranging from alpine meadows to Great Basin Desert. Achieve familiarity with a diverse insect fauna. Learn identification, collection and curation techniques. Conduct field work in a variety of life zones and communities.*

"Wow," I thought: "Bug Camp." My pulse quickened and my heart warmed—signs experience has taught me to heed. "Pay attention," they say. "There's a train coming. If you climb aboard, it will take you on the next adventure of your life."

Most of my book learning about insects has come from children's nature guides—a good starting place for a novice. The more I glean from casual study, the odder it seems that entomology has not claimed a place in school alongside reading, writing, and arithmetic. Insects scoot and soar through the background of every human drama—and more often than most people realize, they take center stage. Humans wouldn't last long without insects. They provide us with products like honey and silk. More essentially, they pollinate plants, disperse seeds, aerate soil, scavenge wastes, and control pests, making themselves ecologically and agriculturally indispensable.

Yet insects can also, of course, be monstrously destructive. Every known plant on Earth serves as lunch for at least one kind of insect. In some agricultural areas, insects regularly devour three-fourths of the crops. Furthermore, by biting and stinging, spreading disease, and destroying homes and possessions, these small creatures inflict large-scale misery.

And they are ubiquitous. Insects inhabit every peak and pocket of the earth's surface, from icy poles to deserts, snowfields to steaming volcanoes. They fly high above the Himalayas and dwell deep in caves. An average-sized back yard may host more than a thousand kinds of insects, each one exploiting a slightly different niche in that small world.

Insects also display remarkable power for their size. Some beetles can lift the proportional equivalent of a sixty-ton object. A grasshopper can leap the length of an insect-scale football field. A flea can spring to a height comparable to that of a thirty-story building. And in terms of technological prowess, insects are the rocket scientists of the nonhuman world. They devised a method of jet propulsion long before we had the wheel. They also invented air conditioning, antifreeze, papermaking, gardening, chemical warfare, celestial navigation, the social division of labor, bait-and-switch advertising, and communication through dance. Who wouldn't want to study these animals?

It's April, and I'm driving east across a hazy Central Valley to the University of California at Davis—the home institution of the field-course instructor, an ant specialist named Phil Ward. After a flurry of e-mails, he has agreed to waive the prerequisite of an introductory entomology course and admit me into his summer class, on the condition that I do some remedial work over the spring. Generously, he has also invited me to visit his lab, so that he can teach me how to collect and study insects on my own.

I exit the interstate onto a long campus drive, passing between hedgerows of native shrubs abloom in California colors: sprays of indigo *Ceanothus* alternating with sunny blossoms of flannelbush. I wonder where this blue-and-gold highway will lead. For me, the summer entomology program offers more than a crash course in insects. It's also a chance to step, for a short while, into the territory of the scientific naturalist.

It seems to be my lot to hover between two oft-estranged worldviews: the outlook of the artist-dreamer and that of the trained biologist. Steeped for twenty years in a life of language, literature, and art, I have never given up the yen for a more measured way of knowing. I admire the scientific investigator's thorough training, her careful rationality, her ability to focus on one question long enough to work out a solution. But I wonder whether I have the requisite mental discipline. I love to learn from books and conversations what scientists have gleaned through patient effort. Set me down in the lab or field, though, and I am prone to daydreaming and dallying. My enchantment with insects springs as much from fancy as from scientific curiosity.

Take the day, several years ago, when I was grieving the end of a mighty love affair. Shared passion for the natural world was a hallmark of this love, and during the long periods of enforced separation that the man and I had to endure, wild creatures—especially insects we had known together—appeared to each of us from time to time in almost startling ways. I could never resist the unscientific temptation to interpret these chance visitations as messages of hope.

Shortly after he and I had parted for the last time, I was at home in my cabin in the woods, dressing for a run. Morning light filtered through the lanky tanbarks outside my bedroom window. On my chest of drawers was a framed photo of the two of us standing arm in arm under a late-summer sky. Flanking the picture sat two small stuffed animals he had given me: a hummingbird and a gecko, both covered in satiny emerald-and-ruby fabric.

Suddenly, I noticed an unfamiliar beetle perched atop the photo frame. Less than half an inch long but spectacularly colored, it sported metallic green wing covers with red highlights and a jewellike sheen. In short, this insect perfectly matched my lover's gifts. While it rested immobile on the picture frame, I fetched my journal.

"I can't avoid feeling that this, too, is an emissary of sorts," I wrote, "and that it brings a message: There will be color and shine, serendipity and surprises yet to come for us, whatever forms they may take."

My field guide tells me that the insect on my dresser that day was a golden buprestid, one of a family of beetles that are often sheathed in metallic colors. This particular member of the family is common in California's coniferous forests, like the stand of redwood and Douglas-fir ringing my cabin. The rationalist in me knew that the creature didn't give a hoot about my love life—but the dreamer took comfort in its arrival.

Of course, people have ascribed personal meanings to the natural world for a very long time. We habitually project our stories onto the rest of nature, seeking omens in the stars and making familiars of the local fauna. Such storytelling has given rise to poetry, art, and mythology. When these narratives spring from attentiveness to natural events, they can help us live well and lightly on the land.

But an unduly human-centered outlook prevents us from learning truths that are essential to the land's survival and to our own well-being. Sentimentalizing about the natural world can backfire when it is uninformed by nature itself. Some well-intentioned activists champion invasive populations of non-native plants or animals, on the grounds that the trespassers are cute or scenic or simply alive. Those who fight to preserve water-hogging blue gum eucalyptus groves in California, for example, have hastened the demise of the coastal scrub on which native wildlife depends—creating silent, impoverished eucalyptus forests where little else grows besides poison oak. Blue gum stands are also notoriously fire-prone: in recognition of their explosive flammability, firefighters refer to the towering Australian imports as "gasoline trees."

As I park my beat-up little Toyota station wagon on the Davis campus, I am hoping that a stint at bug camp will help me think about the insect world in terms more relevant to the insects' lives than to my own. I enter a sprawling building in search of Phil Ward.

The corridors are lined with dozens of doors—many plastered with Gary Larson cartoons, all leading to the offices and labs of insect specialists. Most of these, I later learn, are economic entomologists, or, in professional shorthand, "nozzle-heads": researchers who look for ways to control insects that threaten human health, crops, and profits. With most research funds flowing from big agribusiness, few university entomologists pursue questions about physiology, behavior, evolution, or ecology, apart from commercial implications.

Phil Ward, with his focus on natural history, is a rare exception. An affable man with a trim, dark beard and a relaxed, no-nonsense demeanor, he welcomes me to his lab and gets to business. He patiently describes basic techniques for netting and trapping insects. Next, he shows me how to dispatch my quarry in a killing jar—an ordinary wide-mouthed glass container, inside which a plug of plaster of paris has been allowed to dry. Before depositing live insects into the jar and screwing the lid shut, a collector saturates the plaster with a clear, volatile poison called ethyl acetate. A sufficient quantity will produce fumes that overcome trapped victims quickly, before their struggles can damage wings and other body parts. Too much of the killing agent, though, can soak, stiffen, or discolor the insects, rendering them useless as specimens. I will need practice to get it right.

I knew that studying bugs would entail killing them. Frustrated so far in my attempts to examine insects on the move, I have come to appreciate the uses of a preserved specimen. I even see the value in gathering my own insects rather than using prepared collections. I like being able to recall the smell of the reeds and the sting of sunlight where a damselfly last darted. I am still a reasonably quick learner—but also an alarmingly rapid forgetter. The closer I can get to my subjects in their native habitat, I figure, the more likely I'll hang onto what I learn.

Still, I have not yet made my peace with killing. I picture the giant hand of some extra-terrestrial biologist descending to Earth, in the name of space-alien science, to plunk *me* into a killing jar. What gives me the right to snuff out the spirit of another creature, however small, to assuage my curiosity? An insect's nervous system is far more rudimentary than a person's, but how can I be certain that I am not forcing these tiny animals to suffer as they die?

To his credit, Phil responds respectfully to such questions. Showing no sign of exasperation, he points out that most insects have a short adult life span, often meeting a brutal end in their natural habitat. We collectors, he says, simply add another source of mortality to the mix. Scientific ethics do forbid killing rare or endangered insects. They also dictate minimal disruption of habitats in the process of collecting. As for the subjective experience of a dying insect, says Phil, we can't really know with any certainty—but it probably doesn't suffer.

My misgivings persist, but Phil's reassurances help me rationalize the killing spree on which I am about to embark. I go home to practice collecting insects and then "curating" them for study.

Most specimens can simply be labeled and pinned into the foam-lined bottom of a hinged collecting box. Insects too tiny to pin must first be "point mounted": glued to a teardrop-shaped fragment of stiff rag paper. A few large-winged insects require more elaborate preparation. The butterflies you see in museums and tourist shops, their wings displayed in perfect symmetry, didn't die naturally in that pose. Fresh specimens have to be spread on a special board that's grooved so that the body rests slightly lower than the wings. The collector carefully separates the front and hind wings, using pins and strips of glassine to affix them to the wooden panels of the spreading board. The insect is allowed to dry in this position, then pinned into a foam-lined box.

Delving into the fat entomology text Phil has assigned, I try to master the insect orders—major categories into which insects are grouped. This, Phil has told me, is the bare minimum I must know in order to be ready for his field course. Insects are separated into about twenty-five orders, the most common of these familiar to nonspecialists. There are, for example, the Lepidoptera (scale-wings), or moths and butterflies; the Coleoptera (sheath-wings), or beetles; the Diptera (two-wings), or flies and their relatives. The order Hemiptera (half-wings) includes the stink bugs, bed bugs, and other so-called true bugs. These last are the only insects technically referred to as bugs. But like the rest of us, entomologists in an informal mood use this term for just about any small animal without a backbone.

Besides the more familiar orders, my textbook introduces me to some really far-out groups, such as the Grylloblattaria—literally, "cricket-roaches." Also called rock crawlers, these wingless, mountain-dwelling insects inhabit ice caves, snowfields, and other cold habitats. Not only their weirdness but also their rarity endears them to entomologists. There are only ten species of grylloblattids in all of North America—as compared with tens of thousands of species of beetles in the U.S. and Canada alone.

Despite the best of intentions, I don't get through all of the studying I promised Phil I would do. I arrive at bug camp on a warm afternoon in June, less than ideally prepared. After the six-hour drive from the coast to the mountains with a carpooling classmate, I turn off Highway 89 onto the pleasant dirt road that leads, in two quiet miles, to the field station. A porcupine scuttles into the brush as we arrive. I peel myself from the driver's seat, locate the bedroom that I will be sharing with my one female classmate, and unpack my gear while others straggle in.

Sagehen Creek Field Station occupies eight thousand acres on the eastern slope of the Sierra Nevada, at an elevation of about 6,500 feet above sea level. The cold stream for which it's named flows eastward from the Sierra crest, threading through coniferous forests, marshy meadows, and brushy fields on its way to a reservoir on the Little Truckee River. Shallow and clear, Sagehen Creek slips past the buildings of the field station: a guesthouse with kitchen, dining room, and bedrooms; a few dormitory cabins; a meeting hall; and a rustic laboratory building.

At the introductory pizza dinner, I learn that I am the only student with no formal preparation. My cohort includes a handful of undergraduate entomology majors, a few entomology graduate students, and a couple of professional entomologists. Suddenly, the learning curve I am about to climb rises up before me at a menacing pitch.

The next morning, we get to work collecting insects on the Sagehen property. Already acquainted with the several standard styles of nets designed for sweeping through air, grass, or water, I am introduced to some new equipment. Phil shows us inverted umbrellas for catching insects that fall to the ground when you shake their home shrubs, sifters and funnels for trapping bugs found in soil and debris, baited tents made of nylon netting that imprison flying insects.

My favorite is a contraption that is technically called an aspirator but that everyone refers to as a "pooter." Made for collecting small insects one at a time, it consists of a vial whose cork sprouts two slender tubes side by side—a long, flexible rubber one with a mouthpiece at the outer end and a shorter, rigid one made of glass or plastic. You place the outer end of the rigid tube over the desired insect and literally suck, or "poot," the specimen into the vial. One end of the mouth tube has a mesh covering to prevent a collector from inhaling her own specimens. Phil warns us to avoid using this device near rodent nests, where we might end up pooting a case of hantavirus.

After bouts of collecting, we repair to the dark, concrete-floored lab to identify individual insects. In most cases, there's little hope of naming them down to the species. Each of the major insect orders contains a number of families, and each family embraces multiple genera, which in turn contain various species. Species can differ by literally little more than a hair; you have to be a serious specialist to tell them apart. For each specimen we curate, we are required only to identify the correct family. By the end of the five-week course, each student is expected to produce a tidily labeled and properly organized insect collection representing at least two hundred of the three hundred families of insects that inhabit the region.

When we are not attending lectures or field trips or working on small independent research projects, we bend over dusty lab tables listening to Brazilian CDs on somebody's boom box, sifting through cylindrical cardboard single-serving ice cream cartons containing the day's take, and choosing insects to curate and identify. Phil and his teaching assistant often accompany us, tweezing their own ant specimens out of alcohol-filled vials and rising occasionally to respond to a student's request for help. Day after day, sometimes late into the night, I absorb the banter of this industrious band of bug enthusiasts.

My labmates know a lot, but they are no stodgy scholars. Every few days, one of the guys who's been out collecting runs breathlessly into the lab to shout that a "slave raid" is in progress. Several others, including Phil and the teaching assistant, jump up from their benches to follow the messenger out the door. Though it sounds as if they might be indulging in some frat prank, the gentlemen are actually in hot pursuit of ants.

Along with the termites and some bees and wasps, ants have evolved complex forms of social organization. They live and work together in colonies of up to millions of individuals. Within a colony, two or more generations of adults share living quarters. Males are short-lived drones, while each female colony member is programmed to develop into either a fertile brood producer or a sterile worker.

As a social unit, the colony can accomplish far more than the same number of solitary insects could manage independently. Colonies of social insects may erect towering shelters taller than a person or form bucket brigades to cool overheated nests. They may build living bridges of linked bodies across chasms in their path, assemble armies to overcome adversaries, or muster hunting parties to gather and store huge quantities of food.

Individual ants are dispensable within the colony and useless apart from it. They are replaceable units in a superorganism that draws labor from each according to its ability and provides for each according to its need. As biologist E. O. Wilson wrote in *Journey to the Ants*, "The competitive edge that led to the rise of ants as a world dominant group is their highly developed, self-sacrificial colonial existence. It would appear that socialism really works under some circumstances. Karl Marx just had the wrong species."

There are thousands of ant species and, among them, numerous specialized ways of making a colonial living. Leafcutters of the genus *Atta* harvest tidy bits of greenery with which they nourish fungus gardens that supply food to millions of colony members. Others have cultivated the art of making somebody else do their work. In periodic bursts of energy, these ants raid the nests of a different species, stealing the foreign pupae and hauling them back along a river of hurrying comrades to the mother nest, where the stolen young will be raised up into laborers. When not making raids, slave makers may rely completely on these captured resident aliens to feed and house them and to nurture their own young. It's a local colony of slave-maker ants whose market-day processions periodically draw my compatriots out of the lab at Sagehen Creek.

One day in the lab, a student is pinning an exceptionally large insect: *Stenopelmatus fuscus*, the Jerusalem cricket. It's not a cricket, strictly speaking, but a member of the flightless horned grasshopper family—and it turns out to be none other than the critter I dug up in my back yard a few decades ago. I learn from Powell and Hogue's *California Insects* that this critter burrows in soil, feeding on roots and tubers. Apparently, others before me have reacted in horror on encountering this bug. "No other California insect," write the authors, "inspires such awe. Its large size . . . , spiny legs, giant jaws and, more than anything, its oversized, foreboding, humanoid, bald head, give rise to fear that it is dangerous and even a demon." Nevertheless, they say, the Jerusalem cricket is harmless to humans.

Stenopelmatus is so fat and juicy that, unlike most other local insects, it cannot simply be pinned into a collection box. Specimens this "greasy," says Phil, require taxidermy. So the student makes an incision in his creature's abdomen and eviscerates it. With forceps, he extracts a surprisingly long rope of entrails, which he replaces with a cotton plug before pinning the insect. Several other budding entomologists gather around to enjoy the spectacle.

Along with their gusto for greasy guts, my mostly male classmates exhibit a jockeying, half-joshing competitiveness. This manifests in various ways, including the scorn that they bestow on my ethyl acetate killing jar. The poison of choice among real entomologists, I learn, is cyanide: longer-lasting, faster-acting, easier on wings and other insect features—and far more hazardous to handle.

They also engage in an odd taxonomic chauvinism that I come to think of as "ento-machismo." Some insect orders, it seems, command more respect than others. In this unspoken hierarchy, the status of an order apparently depends on the complexity involved in identifying its constituent species and on the characteristic size and appearance of the insects: the tinier and more obscure, the better.

A student who spends his days preparing and identifying minute specimens of, say, midges or mosquitoes is thus accorded high prestige. Studying these arcane creatures requires heroic hours bent over the dissecting microscope, discerning each family of fly relatives from near look-alikes by examining minute differences in the branching patterns of hairlike wing veins.

In contrast, a lepidopterist can distinguish many specimens of moths and butterflies solely on the basis of habitat, location, and conspicuous markings. Identification of the "leps" therefore often requires nothing more than a specimen in the hand or simply a glance through field glasses. Moreover, the sheer prettiness of these insects attracts everyone from kindergartners to interior decorators. With the objects of their interest frequently sentimentalized by the likes of Hallmark and Disney, lepidopterists sit low indeed on the ento-macho totem pole.

So, although I frequently admire the rainbow of specimens that begins to fill my lep boxes, I succeed only once in engaging one of my labmates in a moment of shared lepidopterophilia. I have just focused my scope on a moth the size of a housefly. Wings that to my naked eye appeared a nondescript tan reveal, under magnification, an intricate geometric pattern of scales, like the weave of a Navajo rug. Their hues range from cream to fawn to burnt umber, highlighted here and there by shining clusters of silver, gold, and copper.

When I invite one of the graduate students to have a look, he peers into my scope and mutters appreciatively. "*Micro*leps," he concedes—meaning the tiny, deceptively plain-looking ones that require a scope for full appreciation— "can be interesting."

One morning, I am leaning over a spreading board, arranging the long, narrow wings of a sphinx moth. With a background color of café au lait, the wings are adorned with elegant stripes in black, white, and Pepto-Bismol. I let out a remark about the creature's striking beauty and am promptly withered by the dour gaze of the student working next to me. "Get over it," his arched eyebrows seem to say. "When it comes to insects, pretty colors are SO not the point."

I can see why my focus on insects' aesthetic appeal might seem, to an entomologist, superficial. If I were tagging along with a crew of otter biologists, I would not expect them to spare much empathy for my unshakable sense of the animals as—well—terminally cute. Deep in their heart of hearts, marine biologists may find otters adorable, blue whales awesome. In their way, my mates in the insect lab no doubt appreciate the beauty of the creatures they study. But perhaps untempered aesthetic and emotional responses can distract from the scientific enterprise, which is, after all, what I have come to bug camp to try to absorb. An entomologist poses useful questions about nature and devises accurate, objective ways of answering them. The best of both worlds, it seems to me, would be to excel at this without losing one's sense of wonder.

The field station lies within reach of a remarkably diverse array of habitats, and on some days we jump into a pair of vans to head for nearby collecting sites. One of our first trips takes us to Butterfly Valley, a marshy haven for exotic-looking carnivorous plants called sundews and pitcher plants, which thrive in the area's acidic soil. I spend a hot, steamy couple of hours collecting dragonflies. These flashy fliers have been clocked at up to thirty-eight miles per hour, and they can hover and change directions instantaneously. Not the best target for a novice net swinger. Finally, I begin to develop some prowess, and in the end I have not only a pair of soggy socks to show for my labors but also an ice cream cup that runneth over with iridescent winged bodies. Then, just before it's time to load up the vans, I make a clumsy move and the open container tips over, spilling its contents irretrievably into the soupy marsh.

My frustration at such moments is intensified by the acquisitive ethos that pervades our class field trips. These outings are intended as forays for tracking down specimens from a variety of distinct habitats, each providing a few unique families toward the required collection of two hundred. Nevertheless, I'm annoyed by the collecting frenzy that arises among my fellow students when we head out into the field. I wield my nets and check my traps amid classmates' cries of "Get it, get it!' "Hey, did you see the belostomatid Phil bagged at Khyburz Flat yesterday? I wish I'd got one!"

Part of me, I admit, buys into the fervor. Beyond the baser competitive greed, collecting mania holds a certain appeal: the thrill of the hunt, the pull of curiosity, the desire to take home insect treasures and examine them closely under the scope. Still as often as not, I don't care about popping one of each thing into the killing jar. I'm more inclined to be led by my curiosity, to watch the insects move and feed and interact. Resentfully, I wonder why I should let a bunch of serious bug people dictate my personal learning style. I can't work up the desire to nab and extinguish a trophy of each significant genus before moving on to the next. And I see in my classmates' cupidity a disturbing tendency to abandon even a shred of appreciation, let alone reverence, for the insect lives that we so freely sacrifice.

But then I have to ask myself whether my disdain for avid collecting might reflect a case of laziness and sour grapes. I wonder if I'm selling myself short by not getting with the program. A collection is a useful tool, after all, and the process of creating it a valuable teacher. Maybe I'm just too undisciplined to accumulate my own two hundred families. I vacillate between two compulsions: stuffing the collecting jar and staring dreamily into the scene.

Finally, it strikes me what an absurd amount of energy I waste by second-guessing myself like this. Ideally, I could embrace both the zeal of the dedicated collector and the reverie of the naturalist and find a way to dance between the two.

I get my opportunity. Two weeks into bug camp, I have to leave for a weekend at home. While I'm away, I miss a group field trip to a high, dry area near the Nevada border—and so, on our next day off, I take myself on a solo outing to the site.

The sun blazes on an open, scrubby landscape electric with the calls of cicadas. I discover that these bugs are a lot easier to hear than to spot. As soon as I isolate the sound of one insect, locate the bush from which it seems to be crooning, and begin creeping in that direction, the canny little creature clams up. I wonder if they can feel the vibrations of my approaching steps. After a half hour of catlike stalking, I somehow manage to nab a cicada. I drop it into my killing jar with the usual mixed feelings, then sit back to eat my lunch and take in the scene. It strikes me that this is one of the best times I've had so far at bug camp and that part of the pleasure has been directing my own insect safari in solitude. I'm on my own, for once, and able to ask questions at my personal pace.

I bet most of my bug camp classmates spent their kidhoods doing just this. They went out into the back yard with a net and a jar and followed their noses. I'm not so different from these guys, I think; I'm just behind them on the learning curve. At heart, they study bugs because they love the whole deal: the fun of trying to figure out what's going on in that wonderfully complex world of small creatures;

the sunburned arms; the quiet sandwich amid the buzz of the high desert on a hot day. Their knowledge has become systematized and the questions they ask more specialized as they've gained expertise, but their enthusiasm still sprouts from the same source. Curiosity isn't a purely scientific or emotional or aesthetic attitude; it's all of these.

When I return to the field station just before dinner, loaded down with nets and jars, the first classmate I see greets me with the familiar cry: "Did you get lots of stuff?' I smile and go inside to put away my gear.

One evening, we trip out to Sand Mountain—a hulking solitary dune alongside Highway 50, whose blue-and-white markers proclaim it the "Loneliest Road in America." We drive east through the Nevada desert: alkaline playas; cattle ranches ripe with the stink of manure; ditches thick with big old cottonwoods, their white fluff flying down the hot, breezy small-town avenues of Fernley and Fallon.

We turn off the highway near a blue booth marked "Loneliest Phone" and arrive, just before sunset, at the Sand Springs Bureau of Land Management Recreation Area and Historic Site. Climbing out of the vehicles, we stand in a wide-open basin ringed by placid skyline. Over our heads lumber a few bruised, gold-edged cumulus. To the east, wispy curtains of pink virga trail over a navy-blue range; from the west, the sunken sun shoots its spokes high into a cloudless pale orange sky. Currents of air, cool at last, caress my sunburned limbs.

As dusk thickens, the instructor and a few students begin setting up equipment for blacklighting. This simple technique involves shining an ultraviolet lamp on a white sheet to bring in insects that are attracted to UV light. We have a similar setup at the field campus most nights. Insects flock to the sheet and remain there until the morning sun warms them into flight. I love stumbling from my cabin into the cold mountain dawn, like a kid to the Christmas tree, to see what we've brought in. In the shadowy morning, the sheet is festooned with an array of colorful moths, some as wide as my palm.

With its pools and vegetation as well as its dune habitat, the area around Sand Springs is known to host a variety of interesting blacklight bugs. As the night deepens, our light draws in a storm of flying creatures. We follow, cooing and exclaiming, forming a press of bodies around the sheet, heads bent over insects pooted and snatched from the melee.

At Sand Springs, I resolve the pull between bug-bagging zeal and dreamy appreciation by gently pushing myself to collect a little more than usual. I get in there with the eager crowd at the blacklight sheet and poot a bunch of small critters. I knock specimens one by one into my jar; an ant lion here, a micromoth there. All around me, a rain of the little back-swimming water bugs called notonectids bounces like popcorn on the sheet. In my light skin and clothing, I am bombarded—ears, hair, shirt—by winged ants, grasshoppers, miniature wasps. I spy a pair of beetles in the act of mating, another beetle munching on its insect prey.

I learn how easy it is to catch a tiger beetle by hand. Only after I have nabbed two or three of these elegant creatures does somebody casually mention that they have a vicious bite. Also after the fact, I hear about the small, yellow, very poisonous scorpions that inhabit the area. It's funny how biting and stinging are probably the first things that occur to most people when they think about close encounters with insects and their invertebrate kin, while it seems to be about the last concern of these bug people. Some of their attitude, I realize, has rubbed off on me. I enjoy my newfound insouciance as we spend field days netting giant bumblebees, tarantula hawks, and other creatures capable of inflicting injury. Aside from a minor ant bite, I've so far escaped painful consequences. If an insect someday does "get" me in a big way—well, maybe it will help me transcend my ambivalence about "getting" insects.

Sometime past nine o'clock, a few of us leave off black-lighting and head up into the sand on foot, toward the beckoning dune. The all-terrain vehicles that zip shrieking through the nearby recreation area by day are mercifully stilled at night. The air remains warm enough for my tank top and shorts.

As we leave vegetation behind and head into the pure smoothness of sand, the act of walking becomes dreamlike. In the dark, our eyes can no longer distinguish sloped planes from level ones. Unable to see the landscape rise or dip or shift alongside us, we race blindly into Sand Mountain's forgiving folds. We know that if we were to fall, the worst we'd face is an unimpeded tumble down the side of a dune. Even running flat out, I feel myself cupped safely in a giant palm of sand.

Beyond the reach of the others' voices now, I clamber up a rise halfway to the crest and find a cradling wall of sand where I lie back just at the angle of repose. The dune's outer skin is cool and silky, losing heat to the night—but a thumb's length beneath the surface, it's hot as a lover's embrace. There's a slight breeze, not hard enough to kick up the fine grains. The moon rises over a silhouetted ridge: slightly orange, gently flattened, a few days past full. Lightning flashes on the horizon; stars shine from a clear window at the zenith.

Snuggling into the dune, I put aside the internal struggle of the past few weeks. I'm grateful for all that bug camp has taught me. I've learned a myriad natural history details and the rudiments of a system for organizing that information. I can tell a bee fly from a blow fly, a tepulid from a tachinid. But more important, I look at the world now through different eyes: more appreciative of the biotic complexity that surrounds and supports us. Studying how scientists measure and interrogate the natural world has helped me to understand how truly immeasurable are its gifts, and how limitless the rewards for those who make scientific scrutiny their life's work. I envision more field courses in my future—today, bugs; tomorrow, bats, hawks, or cottonwood trees.

At the same time, in spite of my science envy, I am not likely to become a scientific researcher. Not in this lifetime. For better or worse, I apprehend the world most readily and most keenly through the eyes of an artist, a writer, a dreamer. And I can't help feeling that, like good science, these ways of knowing may also contribute something essential to healing a tattered Earth.

Those of us who peer at the scientific enterprise from a slight remove, with a mix of admiration, skepticism, and fascination, have our own work to do. Our job is to stay humble and keep learning. Our job is to honor our passion and sharpen our vision. Our job is to communicate with an open heart and all the eloquence we can muster.

My spirits are awake and dreaming—pillowed and buoyed by that benign sand giant. On impulse, I climb to the dune's crest, fling myself over the brink, hit the slope running. Gravity lengthens my stride into a bounding moonwalk, until finally I trip and crumple. Laughing, I curl like a pillbug and let my body roll and roll.

An Incredibly Stupid Flirtation with Death

Being alive is a once-in-a-lifetime opportunity.

—High school student essay

One sunny autumn day, I went hiking in the forest near my home with my friend Eli, a naturalist and passionate mushroom hunter. To his delight, we came across a patch of newly arisen, dinner-plate-sized *Amanita calyptrata* (also called *A. calyptroderma*), a well-known delicacy.

Eli pronounced these the largest specimens of the mushroom he'd ever seen—yet also fresh, tender, and immaculate. Gently brushing off loose redwood duff, he examined several and lifted the best into his collecting basket. When we got back to the house, he left my husband and me with a couple of good-sized mushrooms and a simple recipe.

A couple of hours later, midway through dry-sautéing the diced fungi, I began to have second thoughts. Some *Amanita* mushrooms are infamously toxic. Even though Eli had shown me definitive field marks that distinguish the edible *A. calyptrata* from its lethal cousins—the death cap and the destroying angel, two of the world's deadliest mushrooms—and even though he had sampled this species dozens of times without mishap, I was suddenly plagued by doubt.

What if even Eli had it wrong this one time?

I pulled David Arora's *Mushrooms Demystified* from the shelf. Poring over the *Amanita* section, I learned that the toxic species in this genus cause 90 percent of fatal mushroom poisonings. Arora is not prone to overstatement. He decries the "simplistic slogans" characteristic of some field guides, such as "Do not eat-a the *Amanita!*" He maintains that such injunctions simply "reinforce people's desire for expediency by fostering an unhealthy, mindless reliance on shortcuts and glib generalizations." So his block capitals and exclamation point jumped off the page: "Unless you are ABSOLUTELY, INDISPUTABLY, and IRREFUTABLY sure of your *Amanita*'s identity, don't eat it!"

Moreover, the symptoms of poisoning by the death cap, *A. phalloides*, may not show up for from six to twenty-four hours after ingestion—"by which time," Arora points out, "there is little modern medicine can do except to treat the victim symptomatically."

As I stood at the stove, heavy field guide in my left hand, stirring mushroom pieces over the flame with my right, my husband and I deliberated about whether to toss the pan's contents. The price of prudence would be, at most, an embarrassing moment were Eli to inquire how we liked his mushrooms. The cost of a mistake would be agonizing death. (Arora: "The one adage with which I wholeheartedly concur is: 'When in doubt, throw it out!'")

And so we decided to eat the mushrooms. I'm not sure what this says about us. You might wonder why we would put saving face above ensuring that we could live to see another day. We asked this question ourselves—even as we arranged those tawny chunks on our plates atop mounds of steamed rice.

They were tasty, if not spectacular.

Doing the dishes, we felt fine—but as bedtime approached, we couldn't free ourselves from creeping anxiety. During our evening reading-aloud ritual, we occasionally looked up from the book to exchange nervous glances. ("You still okay?" "I'm okay." "Why did we do this?" "Too late now.")

We climbed into bed with funereal deliberateness—shaking our heads at the folly of our dinner menu, declaring our unconditional love. Both of us were convinced that we might wake up hours later in torment, on our way out of this life. Yet we somehow managed to drift off into a sleep troubled by uneasy dreams.

You're reading this, so you know the outcome. Eli, of course, had not steered us wrong. But how to explain the risk we took?

When we awoke to discover each other breathing and calm, inhaling the cool dawn air, serenaded by mockingbirds and quail, we were flooded with gratitude. Twenty-four hours after what blessedly turned out not to be our last supper, we were dancing giddily around the kitchen. Even now, years after the fact, I occasionally recapture the heart-pounding immediacy of that night of fear and reprieve. In such moments, I experience anew the miracle of being temporarily alive, in this imperfect but serviceable body, on this besieged but astonishing planet, right now.

Perhaps that's what we were after all along: a wake-up call, a reminder to savor every second of this wild and unpredictable life. *Amanita* was our teacher for a day. What some people may accomplish by studying at the feet of a guru, by jumping out of airplanes or by climbing granite walls, we encountered at the end of a fork.

Why Dolphins Help

If . . . the unsubstantiated stories of dolphins pushing humans ashore are true, they must be viewed in the same context as humans pushing stranded dolphins back to sea.

—Richard Connor and Kenneth S. Norris, 1982

My husband and I often walk on a sandy state beach that stretches for many miles along the shore of Monterey Bay. There's always something going on there, from stunt planes barrel-rolling overhead to thousands of Sooty Shearwaters streaming along the horizon on their forty-thousand-mile migration. Occasionally, we're treated to an especially thrilling spectacle: dolphins swimming just offshore. Monterey Bay hosts several dolphin and porpoise species, some of which venture close to land. If we're lucky enough to spot them, it's usually just two or three dark dorsal fins, languidly arcing and submerging. Once in a while, dozens of dolphins speed along in a tight pod, torpedoing in and out of the bay, stitching the surface with frenzied grace.

We aren't the only ones watching. Whenever dolphins appear, human beachgoers cluster along the shore to stare. I suspect that our fellow onlookers share some version of my own mystification: Who *are* those sleek, muscular beings, with their complicated societies and their big mammalian brains? What is it like to be a dolphin, to navigate with flukes and fins and flippers in lieu of arms and legs, to comprehend your surroundings by emitting and receiving sound? What does it feel like when the underwater world to which your species is supremely adapted has become circumscribed by human-made noise, nets, and pollution? Are dolphins aware of us as a threat? As a curiosity? As fellow creatures sharing the planet with them?

Scientists devote careers to such questions, and among the world's most widely respected dolphin researchers is the late Kenneth S. Norris, often called the father of American marine mammalogy. For two decades he was professor of natural history—a rare title in an era of waning academic respect for that interdisciplinary science—at the University of California, Santa Cruz. In 1985, when Norris was still energetically engaged in field research and I was a graduate student in science journalism, I audited his lecture course on marine mammals. Later, a magazine assignment gave me entrée to a couple of hours' audience with him, learning about his research on dolphin societies—a privileged glimpse at the underwater world about which I've so often wondered, through the eyes of an exceptionally keen and erudite observer.

Norris looked avuncular, with a balding pate, slightly rumpled clothes, and an intelligent gaze that projected a beam of mischief. During our interview, I learned that in 1958, he had headed the first crew to bring a live whale into captivity from the open ocean. As he and his colleagues hauled in the struggling young adult female Pacific pilot whale, they watched an accompanying school of Pacific white-sided dolphins attempt to prevent the capture. "Those white-sided dolphins did everything they could think of to try to help that pilot whale get away from us," Norris recalled. "They pressed against the line; they pressed against the whale. They circled the boat for twenty minutes while the whale was up on deck."

Whalers in the nineteenth century witnessed similar occurrences. Whaling crews knew to take advantage of the multiple easy targets provided by whale schools, which would often "stand by" a harpooned schoolmate. Among sailors, whales' dolphin cousins were also known to come to the rescue, in this case helping not only their own kin but also human beings in trouble. Maritime lore is rife with reports of dolphins supporting near-drowning sailors in the water, even guiding them to shore.

Generations-old sailors' tales may not carry the same weight as rigorous observations by the likes of Norris, whose innovative research on whales and dolphins essentially launched the study of cetacean behavior in the United States. (Whales, dolphins, and porpoises make up the animal order Cetacea, from the Greek for "whale.") Nevertheless, so many anecdotes have accumulated over the centuries that at this point nobody doubts the ability of dolphins and toothed whales to give help—to members of other species as well as their own. The question scientists ask now is not whether these animals act altruistically but why, as well as how they do it and what it can tell us about the nature of cetacean societies.

"What the hell are they *doing* out there with that brain? What *are* they doing?" Norris mused when I visited him in his office. The sign on his door read "Norris Aquarium"; he had recently repainted the office walls with an underwater scene.

The question of what cetaceans are up to is understandably tantalizing. Like the higher primates, whales and dolphins have brains comparable to ours in size and complexity; unlike primates, they have no hands, let alone opposable thumbs, and their habitat is both unfamiliar and relatively inaccessible to us. Playing Jane Goodall to marine mammals poses unique challenges. But years of dolphin observation had given Norris and his colleagues some ideas. "I think what they're doing—and I think we're beginning to demonstrate it—is that they have a [social] flexibility imparted by using learned rules and learned relationships—and this almost requires the reciprocal altruistic pattern," he said.

This is the term behavioral ecologists use for a sophisticated form of cooperation found only in animals with highly evolved social systems. To demonstrate this pattern in cetaceans would be to rank them close to ourselves in social complexity. Norris and his colleague Richard Connor laid out the evidence in a 1982 article in *The American Naturalist* entitled "Are Dolphins Reciprocal Altruists?"

In order to qualify as reciprocal, altruistic behavior has to extend beyond close relatives, and it must stand a good chance of being repaid by other members of the society. Although by definition simple altruism does not directly benefit the individual who performs it, most animal societies do reserve altruistic acts for kin. If an individual can save the life of another who shares her genes, she increases the chance of getting some of those genes into the next generation—which in evolutionary terms confers a "selective advantage"; it's a close second best to bearing your own offspring.

But in dolphin society, where an individual may easily associate with a thousand members of its species, saving one's kindness solely for brothers and sisters may be neither practicable nor desirable. Even if the life a dolphin saves turns out by providence to be his second cousin's, the genes shared between the two individuals probably don't amount to enough to compensate the hero for the risks he has incurred or the energy he's expended. His kindness is unlikely to secure a future for his genetic line.

The benefit to a reciprocal altruist comes instead in the assurance that every individual in the society is just as likely to behave altruistically. On some level, every dolphin intuits that its willingness to take care of unrelated "friends" is repaid by a similar willingness on the part of its schoolmates.

"It's so much more valuable to be in a society of friends in the ocean, rather than simply in a family group; the society itself confers selectional advantage on you, every moment of the day, every moment of your life," said Norris. "And you don't have to worry anymore about getting back—because the society is what pays you back. The society does it all the time."

Most of what we know about marine dolphin society fits this model. Groups of animals that are vulnerable to shark attacks need some system of cooperative vigilance—and that's what schools are for. Norris described witnessing this phenomenon in person while doing research with colleague Karen Pryor: "Dolphin schools—the ones we worked with in Hawaii—have got these 'cops' running around. Karen called them *pachucos*, because they look as if they're swinging their chains, you know, in their zoot suits. Most of the time when you come on a dolphin school underwater, you usually see this cadre drive by between you and the other animals."

Research with dolphins has also demonstrated that they are capable of forming abstract concepts—a vital skill if they are to identify animals in distress and provide the appropriate assistance. In one set of experiments performed by Pryor, a rough-toothed dolphin learned to perform various tricks for rewards. Not only did the animal understand requests for specific acts ("Jump through the hoop," "Get the ball"); she also responded, when asked for a "new" behavior, by performing antics her trainers had never seen. Her ability to understand and apply the generalized concept of novelty lends strength to the expectation that dolphins can understand the predicament of a fellow creature in distress.

Dolphin societies show signs of reciprocal altruism through "mutual assistance in combat, in feeding, and in various protective measures [that] members may take either individually or as a group," noted Connor and Norris. For a cooperative system like this to work, however, the society needs some way of preventing freeloading. After all, if you can live among friendly protectors without ever feeling compelled to risk your own neck, you'll probably grow to be the sleekest, most prolific dolphin in the neighborhood. If enough dolphins were to cave in to that temptation, the mutual-aid society would collapse.

This is where big brains become important. As dolphin societies evolved, Norris proposed, somewhere along the way they became "stuck with learning to know a thousand other animals individually and to know whether they trusted them all." To cope with those complex demands, dolphins probably developed a set of subtle social rules, learned by each individual and applied with a flexibility made possible by intelligence.

"It's like what we humans do," he said. "We're constantly checking the validity of our relationships with other individuals. So, like us, dolphins may have responded by building up an ethical society, and the ethics are the rules they refer to. Ethics to me are the learned rules of a society, and in this case, the rules seem to be altruistic."

Yet some apparently altruistic behavior seems so misdirected that it's hard to explain in terms of sophisticated social standards. Female dolphins, for example, will sometimes carry a dead calf around, or in one case even a dead shark, for days on end—hauling it up and down with them on dives. Similarly, pilot whales off Catalina Island have been seen carrying the carcasses of sea lions shot by irritated fishermen competing for their prey. "The pilot whales will carry those things around until all the skin's fallen off them," Norris told me. Fortunately, he added, the whales lack a sense of smell.

Such behavior has led some researchers to suggest that cetacean altruism may be a kind of simplistic response, wired into the genes and triggered by certain stimuli, such as floating dead bodies. But Norris disagreed. Dolphin behavior in general "seems mediated much more by learning than by innate patterns," he and Connor noted in their *American Naturalist* article. When altruism backfires, it may be simply a sign of aberrance, "neurosis," or experimentation on the part of an individual rather than of behavioral rigidity in the entire species.

Norris speculated about how this might work: "Isn't it possible that in a society that runs heavily by learned patterns, there is a certain amount of 'slop'? That is to say, there's a certain amount of freedom for experiment, which is what learning confers. I guess I think the society can get away with it because learning itself implies a dependence on flexibility. *We* seem to function pretty well, even though we do a lot of crazy stuff like that ourselves."

Certainly not all altruistic behavior is easy to understand. What about the dolphins who insist, for example, on supporting an ailing schoolmate at the water's surface for days on end, to the exclusion of their own feeding? "They're so attentive," said Norris. "They'll get up underneath another dolphin and push it to the surface and just keep it there. The only thing they'll do is come up for breath. After about three days of this, you say, 'Gee whiz, don't you want *lunch?!*'" He and his colleagues were at times so worried about the altruistic behavior of some captive dolphins that they relieved the animals of their burdens in order to save their lives.

The tip-of-the-iceberg behaviors that scientists have glimpsed so far only hint at dolphins' complex social world, said Norris. Trying to reconstruct the motivations for altruistic acts from what we've seen is a little like trying to deduce the rules of football by watching a few plays on TV. Part of the problem is logistical. Most of a dolphin's social life takes place underwater—and, as Norris put it, "dolphins don't like divers in scuba gear. They tell you to go to hell when you swim with them. They don't like bubbles, and they don't like to have you coming up underneath them. Perhaps it's because you look like a shark." Also, the trappings and hazards of diving obstruct high-quality science. "I know very few observers who really can function underwater in the ocean very well and come back with observations," Norris said. "Most of the time, most people are worried about themselves. It shuts your mind down. I know, because I tried to observe as a diver for years, and I never, ever got rid of the business of worrying about the sharks behind me."

Norris's innovative answer to these problems was a "new porpoise-watching machine"—successor to an earlier model, the "Semi-Submersible Seasick Machine." The new contraption was a twenty-three-foot overhauled Coast Guard boat, named in Swedish the *Smyg Tittar'n* (loosely translated, "the Tiptoeing Peeping Tom"), in honor of Norris's Swedish graduate student Jan Östman. A person-sized hollow transparent cylinder inside the vessel's hull could be lowered five and a half feet below the water's surface. The researchers would drive the boat to a research site with this chamber in its hoisted-up position and lower it when they arrived. "Jump in with a video camera and recorder," said Norris, "and you can dive with the animals, with 360 degrees of windows to watch from. The boat is much less disturbing to the dolphins than a diver would be."

Norris was "clearing the decks" of some of his teaching and other responsibilities so that he could devote more time to studying dolphin behaviors, particularly those exhibiting altruistic patterns: "There's nothing like getting underwater with dolphins to figure out what their world is like. You can sit there on the surface and talk all day for six weeks, and you still can't imagine what their world is like unless you get your head underwater. All the vistas we've got ahead of us in this behavioral work are really exciting. I feel we have our hands on some things of great importance that will eventually help us understand how people act."

For Norris, elucidating dolphin social behavior meant revealing how much we have in common with them—and, ultimately, with all animals. Dolphin altruism presents a strong case for the notion that nonhuman animals are capable of sophisticated intellectual activities like generalization. Our species doesn't have a monopoly on consciousness, he said. "That's another thing we used to hang onto, saying it was a God-given talent of humans. Baloney! It's probably a God-given talent of a great many animals."

He got up, made a brief tour of his office, and returned to the chair where he had been sitting. "During that little traverse I took," he said, "I had enormous amounts of information come in to me: the colors of the desk, the shapes, the points, the whole shot. Most of it was irrelevant to me. But I did worry about [tripping over] your foot, and I didn't want to get stuck in the corner. I had to make generalizations to avoid various things. I threw away a billion bits in the process, and I picked out the relevant ones.

"Does a bee do that? I don't know—how the hell does a bee get around if a bee doesn't do that? Is consciousness implicit in that set of actions? Well, I say somewhere in there, in some animals below human level, consciousness is implicit.

"I suspect that the first signs of consciousness are going to be found very far down in the animal kingdom. Every move we make as biologists is forcing us to recognize how we are not special. We are, in fact, a seamless part of the living world, with no break or barrier at all.

"I don't think I'm ever going to see very far under the hem of nature's garment at . . . what a terrible metaphor!" Norris grimaced, laughed, tried again. "I think the complexity is going to march ahead of us—when we look at bird behavior, when we look at fish, at turtles, at insects—until the whole lineage becomes quite seamless. That's what I think."

Ken Norris's cetacean research generated unprecedented insights about whales and dolphins and their social interactions and echolocation abilities. Norris died in 1998, and many of the questions he posed about marine mammals are still a long way from being answered. His colleague Richard Connor noted in a 2010 email exchange with me that theories about cooperation and altruism among animals have "evolved immensely" in the decades since he and Norris published their 1982 paper. In the absence of direct evidence, Connor is skeptical about whether a system of reciprocal altruism, in the strictest sense, operates in dolphin communities; he and others have proposed alternative hypotheses. "We still don't know," he says, "but dolphins"—with their complicated and fascinating systems of cooperation—"are still the best place to look."

Connor and his fellow investigators continue to devise new ways of watching dolphins up close, seeking plausible explanations of their behaviors and interactions. The rest of us keep on staring out from shore and peering over boat railings, full of wonder and unanswered questions, yearning for contact with our alluring, alien kin.

Confluence: A Bit of Eco-Erotica

High on a Southwestern plateau, two rivers plow converging canyons. From headwaters two hundred miles apart, they slide and tumble toward each other, carving out of the red earth between them a great southward-thrusting wedge of desert. At the apex of this tapered mound, the rivers meet.

They come together as strangers, each carrying the memory of its own coursing, braided journey. Flowing toward the confluence from the northwest, the Green River meanders through languid bends, looping extravagantly on itself like a sated snake. It laps at heat-bleached gravel bars and cottonwood banks; it eddies in shaded spring-fed grottoes cushioned with saturated moss. Electric-blue damselflies needle its oily currents. The Green reaches its rendezvous perfumed with the sunny, watery scents of willow and butterscotch weed.

From the northeast, the swollen Colorado rides heavily, engorged with the red-brown silt of calving sandstone cliffs. As it rounds the mesa, it is surprised in a surge of tidal confusion by the Green. The two rivers spill into one broad southbound waterway. Shuddering gently over the same shallow bed, their waters slip together. Alien currents merge; contrasting temperatures mingle. Under the surface, jade sweetwater rivulets meet clay-smooth tongues thick with iron sediment. In a roiling embrace, the new partners move onward.

At first, their progress is tentative and leisurely. The water's tranquil pace seems almost stilled, suspending time. Yet rising up the canyon, from some distant point downstream, echoes the thunder of a great falling. There is no turning back.

Gradually, the canyon narrows and deepens, and the entwined rivers quicken in a tightening embrace. Standing waves vibrate the walls in a rhythm that resonates more deeply than sound. Twigs and other bits of floating debris ride the surface, pausing atop each glassy swell before twitching off to slide into the trough and over the next rise. Protruding rocks create chutes and rills; whirlpools gather spiral strength, sucking in counterpoint to the current's momentum.

The rivers cry out as they accelerate in their conjugal bed, their thin resistance overwhelmed by a rumbling hunger for sea level. The canyon floor drops more steeply. The water surges forward, a white madness now, bucking and writhing. Mingled among the riverine voices are high, splashing, plaintive notes, guttural gurgles, moans and roars that swell and recede and swell again. The torrent has become a single thrashing beast that speaks to itself—crooning, pleading, urging, commanding. The bouncing current slaps against slickrock walls, glazing the thirsty stone with a shining film. Boulders toss the water wildly upward as it storms through its confining channel.

Then suddenly the walls burst outward and the bottom falls away. The river explodes into sky, pausing airborne for a frozen moment. A fizzing curtain of mist shatters the sunlight into colored splinters. Freightloads of water drop over the precipice to the rocky shelf a hundred feet below, where the impact churns the waters white again and sends them diving in a series of frothing cascades.

Finally, these gather into one narrow waterfall, the last. As if poured from a high-held pitcher, it plummets, chortling, into a deep hollow, where the waters pool in green shadow. Bubbles rise and dissolve as the wild crashing above recedes into sleepy memory. Quieted and calmed, murmuring tenderly, the united rivers slip downstream over the brink of their gentle pool, toward the untasted twists and drops of a thousand more riverbed miles.

Coming around the Bend:
Why We Need the Unexpected

Our ordinary surroundings, built and natural alike, have an immediate and a continuing effect on the way we feel and act, and on our health and intelligence.

—Tony Hiss

When I was in my teens, I came upon John Muir's description of his first glimpse across California's Central Valley, from the grassy crest of the Coast Range to the granite peaks of the Sierra Nevada. Standing at the summit of Pacheco Pass in April, facing east, Muir looked over a sea of wildflowers that stretched to the north and south farther than he could see. Nearly a hundred miles ahead, the Sierra rose from a belt of pink and yellow foothills into purple mountains capped with a pearl-gray frosting of snow: "a wall of light ineffably fine," he wrote, "and as beautiful as a rainbow."

Reading Muir's passage, I recalled riding inland from Berkeley toward the mountains in my family's car. We would wind gently up the coastal slopes until, coming around a bend in the highway, we reached a vantage point similar to Muir's. Peering eastward through yellow-gray smog, I beheld the great valley below, plowed and platted, the Sierra a dirty mirage in the distance. My spirits sank at the sight. Only about a century had passed between Muir's viewing and mine; the contrast attested to rapid and violent changes in the California landscape.

Years later, I taught a group of ten-year-old girls in an after-school nature notebook workshop. On the first day, as we introduced ourselves, I asked them to think out loud about "nature." What exactly does the word mean? What is natural and what is not? After the girls had talked for a while, I asked whether they considered human beings a part of nature. "We used to be," volunteered one of the young students, "but we domesticated ourselves."

Wielders of combines and chain saws, bulldozers and backhoes, we in the developed world have indeed domesticated ourselves and our surroundings—and now we are asking, with increasing urgency, what we have lost. Among the spiritual satisfactions we forfeit when we tame the landscape is that of coming around a bend, as John Muir did when he topped Pacheco Pass for the first time, and discovering something wide open and wild. Muir tried to keep his contemporaries from closing in on the last of the untrammeled places. Today, denizens of the American West struggle to hold back development from a few remaining relatively wild public lands—what Wallace Stegner called the geography of hope—in order to preserve not only the land but also a pioneer's sense of limitless possibility within ourselves.

Towns and cities cannot substitute for wilderness—neither ecologically nor as shapers of character and aesthetic sensibility. Yet even urban areas can offer moments of private pioneering, an uplifting sort of coming-around-the-bend.

One morning I found myself in an unfamiliar neighborhood within a mile of my home, on a side street where I'd never walked before. I could hear the traffic a few blocks away at the grocery store where I shop every weekend, but I couldn't picture my position in relation to other streets, and suddenly I had no idea what lay around the next corner. In a small way, I was lost.

With the disorientation came unanticipated pleasure. I had no mental map for this place, no internal photograph of what to expect as I gazed down the winding street. I became elated, charged with a sense of adventure. If I didn't know what waited around the bend, anything might greet me there—a spectacular flower garden, a funky Victorian cottage, the season's best blooming eucalyptus, a stranger who would end up a friend. I found myself savoring the moment and reluctant to return to familiar ground.

This brief encounter with the unpredictable echoed experiences I've had on the trail and the road, and it illuminated one reason why I love to travel. Visiting a place for the first time, whether a mountain river or a roaring city, makes almost everything worth examining, given that very little is dismissibly familiar. When one is unable to slip the scene into a comfortable context of memory, the senses open up to every stimulus. The world is new.

As I wandered my own stretch of urban frontier that morning, I wondered what it would take to cultivate a traveler's openness, even amid the dailiness of home. Some artists, dreamers, and spiritual practitioners manage to sustain the ability to see their surroundings in this way, while the more demoralized among us have lost faith in the idea that something unexpected and rejuvenating could lie just around the corner. Most people's outlook swings between those extremes of glum indifference and expectant curiosity. Which perspective dominates depends on the environments where we live and work—the shapes, smells, textures, and colors of the spaces we encounter every day.

Although we have lost the literal frontier, we haven't shed our need for the inviting, unknown place that lies just ahead. Most of us live in cities, so preserving wilderness areas and establishing national parks, though essential, are not enough. How can we create more inviting spaces close to home—to everyone's homes, not just those of the wealthy—that offer a sense of mystery and promise and that elevate rather than diminish our spirits? Public gardens, playgrounds, and pathways; restored riverfronts; pedestrian malls; museums and cathedrals—many kinds of city places have that power. I once toured a large college dormitory whose designer had introduced sinuous curves into the building's long corridors. His innovation resulted in a series of rounded alcoves with limited sight lines, lending the public spaces outside the bedrooms a sense of homey intimacy—far more welcoming than a typical dorm hallway.

The most magical urban spaces of all, at least to me, are bookstores and libraries. If I were an architect or planner, I would pay close attention to the places where books are bought and borrowed. Buildings that house books unite two kinds of architecture—literal and literary—and I suspect they can teach us a lot about how to create environments full of hope and good will.

When it comes to design and furnishing, the best book places are tuned to their local communities, with unique signature touches: the parquet floor, the vaulted ceiling, the picture window with a view over the harbor, the brick reading nook filled with cushions, the loft hung with photographs of visiting writers from over the years, the rocking horse in the children's section. But interwoven with the arrangement of physical space is a more complex design—one that changes with the inventory and varies with each visitor, composed of invisible lines of ideas that interconnect books and browsers. In the best, one-of-a-kind bookshops, as in the most enticing outdoor landscapes, mystery and possibility are written into every corner.

One of my favorite local bookstores used to sell a sweatshirt emblazoned with a line from Vincent Van Gogh: "I think that I still have it in my heart someday to paint a bookshop with the front yellow and pink in the evening . . . like a light in the midst of darkness." I don't know whether Van

Gogh ever painted his bookshop, but if he did, it would have been a Bookshop Santa Cruz or an Elliott Bay Book Company, not a franchised, sterilized, predictable space where the electronic cash register resounds more loudly than the thoughts of the browsers.

As a society, we can create surroundings that encourage joyful creativity in each of us—or the kind that drive us to depression. Someone who grows up in a bleak neighborhood accustomed to fearing danger around the corner will have a hard time trusting in the world's miracles. Those who plan neighborhoods and commercial streets, who design buildings and parks, don't determine everything about our surroundings, but they do have tremendous power to influence our attitudes by shaping our physical world.

Domesticating ourselves doesn't have to be a deadly process. We can plant splashes of unexpected color and scent in our cities and build hundred-mile trails around and out of them. We can restore urban waterways, plant rooftop gardens, fund art on the streets, support farmers' markets, make resting alcoves and mini-parks along crowded boulevards, create tree buffers to temper the noise, heat, and danger alongside pedestrian walkways, and push for bike paths and public transportation and cleaner air. And we can support independent booksellers and local libraries in every kind of neighborhood. Whether from Van Gogh's illuminated bookshop window or Muir's luminous wall of mountains, we need the light of hope, discovery, and possibility to shine on the places where we carry out our lives.

Musical Medicine

Healing? I think that's what music is all about. Don't you?

—Yo-Yo Ma

I stood in the wings of a blues show—low light, black and red velvet. My belly glowed in musical empathy. From the sidelines, I began singing along with the soloist—just belting it out. Somebody glanced at me with raised eyebrows—"Are you sure that's permissible?" But I wasn't bothered. What a comfort not to worry about the sound but rather to have faith that since it felt so right, it sounded fine. I was full of soul, full of voice.

I awoke from that dream released from a month's accumulated tensions and freed from a constricting self-consciousness about my voice. I remembered the pleasure of singing without trying to impress. The experience renewed my longstanding curiosity about the power of relaxed singing: the way it works a kind of medicine on body and soul.

It's not a new subject. More than a century ago, choirmaster and singing teacher Leo Kofler studied the physiology of tone production and breathing and discovered that through singing regularly in the right way, he could transform his consumptive condition into a state of robust health.

"But the greatest satisfaction I find," Kofler wrote in *The Art of Breathing* in 1897, "is in the delightful results which my system of voice-production achieves in my pupils. As soon as a pupil has mastered the difficulties . . . of keeping the throat . . . relaxed and free . . . then the voice will at once show an incredible improvement. . . . Men or women with stooping shoulders, sunken chests, and hollow cheeks can, in a few months, become straight, hold the shoulders back and have round chests and a healthy color in their faces."

For centuries, probably millennia, midwives and healers, cantors and Camp Fire girls have noticed the salubrious effects of singing, though Western medicine and physiology have devoted relatively little study to the hows or the whys. "Singing makes you healthy, and singing is a sign of good health," proclaimed a scientist delivering a paper to a 1981 seminar on singing research at the Swedish Academy of Music. But he followed this promising introduction with apologies about the paltry supporting data he could provide.

People who tap the healing power of song abound in holistic health circles. These practitioners don't usually explain their work in terms of physiology, though, which frustrates the biology student in me: I want to be able to visualize specifically *what* is happening inside me when singing makes me feel better—and *how* I can get it to happen more often. Sound healers tend to draw instead on spiritual metaphors about tuning in to the vibrations of the cosmos. If they talk about physical effects, it's in loose terms.

"In chanting, you circulate the breath, harmonize the vibration of cells, organs, molecules, brain rhythms. . . . Sound has a very powerful effect on the body," says Jill Purce, a teacher of workshops on sound and healing. "Making the body sound, or feeling in tune, so that we're not highly strung: all these musical terms that we find in our vocabulary point towards a kind of musical medicine."

Purce, the daughter of a concert pianist and a doctor, studied meditative chanting with Tibetan and Mongolian monks and has taught this and other musical techniques in popular workshops. "The single greatest cause of illness is regret and anxiety," Purce declares. "The cure for that is to think of some way that we can be fully in the present."

To distract the mind from its usual "internal chattering," she has people practice the ancient technique of harmonic overtone chanting. This involves singing a single note and then, by carefully altering the shape of the vocal chamber, splitting the note into harmonic overtones much the way a prism breaks white light into spectral colors. The pure, fluty tones that float magically above the fundamental note of a practiced chanter create a kind of acoustic rainbow.

"I had a sense of something hidden, dark, black, very disturbing," says one woman of her experience working with Purce. "It's a feeling of grief I've known since I've been a child, and I've never been able to pinpoint it. Gradually . . . I could visualize and verbalize it to Jill. Just very recently I've actually been able to really uncover what the problem was, and I'm absolutely sure the deepest wound that I've known since I was a child has actually gone now. I have been able to let it go and have something else in its place, which is joy rather than pain."

Musician and sound healer Kay Gardner suggests one possible bridge between work like Purce's, which has its roots in mystical traditions, and physiological models that the stubborn, just-the-facts-ma'am side of my brain can accept. She notes that the medical technique of destroying kidney stones with ultrasound vibrations may not be so different from one sound healer's reportedly successful attempts to sing away her own benign tumor.

Beyond singing's good vibrations, music has additional charms to soothe a savage breast—and many realms of body and mind. Neuroscientists have observed, for example, that musical training seems to improve people's skills in other areas, such as reading—one good reason to prioritize music instruction in schools. Researchers working with stroke victims have known for some time that the one in five stroke sufferers who are no longer able to speak can usually still sing. (Similarly, stutterers become fluent when they sing lyrics instead of speaking sentences.) Now, by having stroke patients match their verbal phrases to rhythmic melodies, these scientists are using the brain's "singing center" as a byway back to speech. Other research demonstrates that music's rhythmic quality can help loosen the halting or frozen movements of people with Parkinson's disease.

Clinical research has shown that singing can help people suffering from Alzheimer's and other forms of dementia temporarily recover lost memories. Pediatrics researchers who played soft Mozart in an Israeli neonatal unit observed that it seemed to speed weight gain in premature infants. And a Swedish study suggested that women serenaded by musical recordings while under general anesthesia during surgery tended to recover sooner and with less pain than those without benefit of music.

As effects like these become better understood, the field of "music therapy" is gaining respect. Currently, a few thousand registered practitioners, with advanced training in both music and psychology, are plying this trade. In some medical settings, such as the Mayo Clinic's cardiovascular surgery unit in Rochester, Minnesota, music therapists employ music as part of a recovery program, citing its power to reduce stress and improve moods.

Someday, when evidence-based scientific explanations for music's healing powers have matured, they may meet up with spiritual understanding, until, ultimately, we stop seeing a sharp distinction between these ways of knowing. Balfour

Mount, a medical doctor and professor of palliative medicine at McGill University, has observed that healing is at root an arrival "into the present moment." It entails a shifting of our frame of reference from head to heart, he says—a dissolving of barriers between ourselves and others, between ourselves and the wider world. Mount wrote in 2004 that "music, when it is truly healing, may . . . cut through our carefully constructed defenses, thus liberating a deeper appreciation of mystery and the potential for healing that lies within. . . . Perhaps, in its vibratory nature, music opens us to a greater appreciation of our essential connectedness to the cosmos, our oneness with all that is."

My voice rises from a glow inside my trunk. I relax and admit sweet breath into my body, then feel the muscles of my abdomen, back, and chest contract and my limbs vibrate as the air resonates. The song is a warm river flowing, breaking apart icebergs of daily fear and uncertainty. I feel strong and powerful as I make beautiful liquid sounds. I don't think about my throat or mouth or about sounding good.

In harmony with the voices of friends, this kind of singing is magical. When doctors are more enlightened, they will write prescriptions for it. One thing is clear: for singing to heal, it must not be about performance. All of the teachers, healers, and singers I've consulted insist that anyone with a voice, no matter what they've been told about its quality, can learn to experience power, joy, and release in song.

Cupid's Chemistry

We've read it in classical mythology, heard it in popular songs, seen it on Saturday morning cartoons. What more evocative metaphor for erotic attraction than the image of Cupid shooting victims with potion-tipped arrows? Changes cascade through a smitten lover as if triggered by a drug—often unbidden and usually resistant to willful control. When that concoction from the little archer's quiver gets under your skin, a warm pressure rises in your chest until you draw sweet, sighing breaths. Your hands and lips crave touch; your belly glows like hot coals; your blood is spiced with the clove-and-orange oil of desire.

For decades, scientists have been examining Cupid's quiver in search of a formula for romantic love. Biochemists, physiologists, affective neuroscientists—those who study the neural bases of emotion—offer tentative descriptions of what happens inside and between people who are drawn or devoted to each other. Romantic crushes, erotic yearnings, and serious loves have colored and shaped my life, and I have plenty of questions about the hows and whys. At the same time, I find myself pondering just what it means to *explain* a human emotion.

What was it that caused me to fixate, for example, on that one particular boy in high school? I'll call him Ben. With warm eyes, long brown locks, and a trim beard, he was nice-enough-looking, though he wasn't the handsomest or most engaging guy in school. But he was a gifted, passionate jazz musician, and my whole being opened in moist, feverish longing whenever I heard him play. I loved the way he lost himself in improvised solos, closing his eyes and throwing his head back without a hint of self-consciousness. I obsessed about him daily, spilling out my lonely desire in desperate verse. I had boyfriends during that time, but none who filled me with the same pulsing desire. Too shy to pursue Ben actively, unprepared at sixteen to bring a thundering erotic hunger into an actual relationship, I remained intoxicated by the thought of him for a good two years. It didn't matter that we never really got to know each other. Or was it *because* we remained near strangers that I couldn't get over my crush?

A couple of years ago, in a moment of curiosity, I googled Ben's name and learned that he had recently recorded an album of his own compositions. I downloaded a couple of tunes and discovered that decades later—after several dalliances, a few serious relationships, and fifteen happy years with the love of my life—a few phrases from Ben's piano have the power to excite me even now. The scientific explanation for this has got to be interesting—if in fact it can ever be spelled out.

Paradoxically, some of the most interesting insights about love chemistry come from observations of people who exhibit extreme forms of emotional behavior. So-called "love-blind" individuals, for example, are unable to develop a crush on the girl or boy next door any more than someone with red-green color blindness can visually distinguish lime lollipops from cherry ones. A Johns Hopkins researcher who worked with more than twenty such people hypothesized that damage to certain nerve pathways in their brains prevents the release or proper reception of chemical compounds involved in attraction. While people afflicted with this rare condition may be perfectly sociable and do sometimes form long-term emotional partnerships for the sake of affection and companionship, they are strangers to heartache and passion.

Not so "attraction junkies," who initiate one relationship after another in whirlwind pursuit of infatuation's heady rush. Their ardor is fueled, research suggests, by addiction to phenylethylamine: an amphetamine-like neurotransmitter that we produce in large amounts during the early stages of a love affair. It boosts euphoria, optimism, and energy. And then there is the "attachment junkie," who experiences extreme anxiety or depression when separated from his or her long-term partner, forced to do without the physiochemical soup that the relationship cooks up.

The similarity of such experiences to those of drug addicts has prompted research into the chemical imbalances that may engender love addictions. From these studies has come some initial understanding of the neurological underpinnings of love and attraction in "normal" people. For example, evidence suggests that when contented couples get together, their brains produce pleasing amounts of opioids—compounds chemically similar to the narcotic alkaloids that are produced by the opium poppy and serve as the basis for drugs like morphine, codeine, heroin, oxycodone, and other addictive painkillers. A UCLA study showed that holding hands with or even just gazing at a beloved partner—or their mere *photograph*—can reduce pain from an illness or injury, just as injecting or ingesting a plant-based opiate can do. Investigations into the chemistry of devoted love suggest that harmonious long-term relationships boost the body's production of these natural feel-good chemicals, or endorphins (*endo* for endogenous, or internally generated; *orphin* for morphine-like substance)—which have the power not only to mute pain but also to enhance immune function, blood circulation, and emotional well-being.

Research on love and desire tends to focus on heterosexual relationships, though some studies pay attention to same-sex attractions. Straight women and gay men who are exposed to the smell of men's sweat appear to respond with endocrine secretions in their own bodies. Researchers have identified the responsible chemical as androstadienone, a male sweat component that gets picked up by the subjects' olfactory systems and then, the scientists propose, stimulates a chain of neurological changes. If this is true, it places androstadienone in the category of that sought-after grail, the bona fide human pheromone. Some purveyors of men's fragrances now peddle androstadienone-containing colognes, claiming their products can help the wearer catch a woman.

There's a lot more to perspiration than meets the nose— more than we had even begun to realize before scientists started paying close attention. Some people's sweaty aromas appeal to us more than others, and researchers in Australia have found that these preferences may have evolved to help us conceive healthy children. The scientists propose that chemical signals in a woman's sweat tell a potential mate whether the couple's offspring would be likely to have strong immune systems. The more promising the woman's genetic immune makeup, or histocompatibility complex, the more alluring she smells to him. Earlier research showed that couples tend to be most attracted to each other when their sweat smells differ most distinctly. Over the course of evolution, this may have helped guard against matings between genetically related, or unrelated but too-similar, individuals.

Biological anthropologist Helen Fisher, a specialist in the science of love, told CBS that "affairs of the heart are often functions of the brain." And Joni Mitchell observed in an interview several decades into her songwriting career, "I'm hip to romantic love: it's a trick of nature." Like skeptics peering closely at the magician's hand, scientists are trying to remove the mystery from that trick. But explaining love and desire in physical and evolutionary terms is one thing, *understanding* it another. Scientists are limited to studying the measurable; we may never be able to quantify some aspects of emotion or sexuality. And when we elucidate passion through the lens of neurochemical pathways and hormone cycles, we risk reducing romance to those images alone. Philosopher Aldous Huxley called this syndrome "nothing but" thinking, which understands human beings as "nothing but bodies . . . even machines."

When I was little, I had a plastic doll whose makers called her Chatty Cathy. When you pulled a string emanating from Cathy's navel, she introduced herself or invited you over for tea. (Why my parents entrusted her to me I don't know, since they had already witnessed my destructively zealous scientific curiosity when I hurled the family Etch A Sketch off my sister's top bunk to reveal its contents.) One afternoon, intrigued, I hacked a hole in Cathy's perforated breast, shone my flashlight on her innards, and there discovered the mechanical basis of my doll's gift for gab.

Had I taken the little metal box mounted there for all of Cathy, I might have felt the magic slowly slink out of our relationship. But instead of becoming nothing but a tape recorder in my eyes, the doll also remained a companion and comforter—open heart surgery and all. Her "Cathy-ness" consisted of much more than the machinery that made her talk.

So it is with the science of love. No harm lies in illuminating the neurochemical "machinery" that turns a lover's crank, so to speak, when her current heartthrob walks by.

Understanding the physical changes that underlie or accompany emotional states may help us navigate the choppy
waters of romantic love more effectively—for example, by
showing us ways to keep the "chemistry" alive in a long-term
relationship. Scientific models may well take their place beside psychological, sociological, spiritual, political, and metaphorical ways of knowing love. But I doubt the researchers
will ever replace those ways of knowing; it's just too hard to
write a good song about phenylethylamine.

DRAWING LESSONS

Eyes of the World

Your job is to find what the world is trying to be.

—William Stafford

On a gray New England day, two dozen college class-mates and I sat at long wooden tables in a basement biology lab, serenaded by clanking radiators. Hunching over micro-scopes, we examined bits of greenery.

On the stage of my scope lay the feather-shaped frond of a fern. Along its pale green underside, the frond's pro-jecting fingers were studded with brown, BB-sized dots. As I turned the focusing knobs, each dot gradually resolved into a mounded cluster of tiny, translucent umber globes glowing faintly in the beam of the scope's bright lamp.

My first two years of college had been fraught with am-bivalence. Lacking confidence in my training and aptitude, I initially shied away from the science classes that intrigued me. Instead, I sought fulfillment in music and activism, friendship and romance. Soon I was spreading my energies so thin that no one pursuit brought satisfaction.

But all the while, there was running through my days an-other sort of extracurricular experience—a private, inexo-rable one that I never thought of as pertinent to my educa-tion: I *noticed* and *felt* my everyday world with great intensity. A walk from dorm to classroom down a leaf-strewn sidewalk on a late-fall day, past chittering squirrels, doorway cats, and strolling crowds, could fill me to overflowing with sensations and questions. The quality of light slanting through a dining hall window, the scents of a grimy working-class neighborhood where I bought groceries, the clatter of a subway car out of subterranean grit into a golden winter afternoon—I found these more provocative than the formal features of my college life.

At the time, this oddly receptive turn of mind didn't strike me as an academic asset. In childhood, I'd often been accused of oversensitivity; in college, my tendency to be stirred by such a wide range of stimuli seemed an embarrassing liability, a form of romanticism that distracted me from concerted learning. I couldn't seem to discover a bridge between my sensory suggestibility and a recognized course of study. I often found myself more interested in *being* than *doing*—a predilection unlikely to land me on the dean's list.

What I couldn't yet appreciate is that the capacity to simply *attend* is a gift. It can give rise to creativity and joy, as well as intellectual engagement; it can foster a life of reverence, compassion, and useful work. But to reap such rewards, one must learn to temper wonder with knowledge, curiosity with method. And here, one of my first teachers was the underside of a fern.

Before taking this introductory botany course, I had never turned over the foliage of a fern, never noticed the intricate structures that decorate specialized fronds. Now, despite the unfamiliarity of new terms and concepts, studying plants was beginning to feel like coming home.

As I set to work in the lab that autumn afternoon, I knew that each of the minute capsules clinging in rounded clumps to my scrap of foliage contained countless spores—microscopic fern factories. Ferns, more primitive than flowering plants, cannot produce seeds. Instead, they play out a two-stage reproductive process. First, the plants we normally recognize as ferns release spores, which land on the earth and develop into stubby, inconspicuous plantlets. Wherever fern plants grow and multiply, these low-growing protoferns also appear, though at three or four to the linear inch, they're easy to overlook.

Every plantlet produces both eggs and sperm cells. If the ground becomes moist enough, the sperm begin to swim egg-ward, like sperm the world over, toward a rendezvous with fertilization. Each successfully mated pair of sex cells then grows into a young fern plant, which eventually develops spore-bearing structures, and the cycle begins again.

The course instructors required us to sketch everything we observed in the lab. It didn't matter, they assured us, how well we could draw. They simply wanted us to look long and hard enough to make visual notes. I'd always envied people who could translate their seeing with artful precision into lines, shapes, and shadows on paper—and while I didn't imagine I could ever join their ranks, I was intrigued by the explicit permission to draw without regard for artistic ability. So I scrutinized the clusters of spore capsules that clung to the fern's nether parts, tracing their contours on a notebook page. Absorbed in that delicate caress, I channeled aware-ness from eyes to hand to paper. To my surprise, the resulting sketches bristled with life and, if not scientific accuracy, at least a pleasing authenticity.

As I stared, the scene under my microscope came to life. A puff of what appeared to be brown smoke materialized in the air over the frond, momentarily obscuring my view. At first I was mystified; then it dawned on me what must be hap-pening. One of the tiny capsules, drying in the heat of the scope's lamp, had burst open to release a swirling cloud of near-weightless microscopic spores. As the first puff of spore dust began to disperse, another appeared nearby. Soon, one hollow capsule after another was letting loose. Miniature pandemonium broke out under the magnifying lenses, spore capsules exploding like popcorn all over the smoking brown field of the microscope stage. If my hearing were acute enough and rightly tuned, I wondered, would the room fill with wild and unfamiliar sounds?

In their native habitat, those spores would disperse on the slightest current of air, gradually settling over a broad swath of ground; some would eventually give rise to a new generation of ferns. In the lab, another kind of germination was taking place. I annotated the growing sketch in my notebook. And as I watched and drew and wrote, a quiet but insistent happiness began to bloom, along with the shifting whorls of fern futures that danced beneath my gaze. Witnessing the fern's display, I entered into a state of alert, focused *presence*. My senses sharpened; my mind clarified; my body became serene and awake. I associated such attunement with long walks, with dabblings in poetry and calligraphy and other private ventures. Now, finally, I was experiencing it in a classroom.

That an event of such seemingly modest proportions could engender this happy state—and that I should remember the moment so vividly thirty years later—attests to the potency of natural history study, not only as a way of learning how life works but also as a path to fuller living.

Some of the quiet joy I felt in the lab that day arose from a welcome dose of humility. The college I attended had a long history of hubris and self-congratulation and an institutional cosmology that placed human affairs at the center of the universe. At the onset of an epic blizzard that beset New England during the winter of my junior year, one administrator intoned in response to a reporter's question, "Harvard *never* closes, not even for an act of God." (Divine intervention or no, the university did indeed shut down for several days a short while later.) Here under my microscope was an elegantly orchestrated phenomenon, one of a myriad, that had been playing out around me all my life—and for millions of years before humans showed up on the planet. In pointing to an ancient, intricate world that extended profoundly beyond my own small self, the fern's display offered a refreshing perspective.

And while it's true the plant had no need of me, we were, nevertheless, kin. Fern gazing offered a glimpse into universal, elemental life processes that link human beings with every other organism on the planet. To witness such events in action is to be reminded of one's membership in the community of life. Nature close at hand offers a lesson in both the simple logic that compels so much of biological activity—*Be fruitful and multiply*—and the staggering complexity entailed in carrying out that imperative at the level of cells and molecules.

Such complexity invited inquiry. What mechanism caused the spore capsules to burst open under the heat of the lamp and propel their contents outward? How much heat was required? How many spores swirled in each of those minute dust clouds, and why such abundance? Did other forest creatures make use of the spores—make them into fertilizer, eat them for lunch? In the woods, how far could a single spore travel? How many spores might succeed in dividing and developing into protoferns, in turn creating new fern plants? I could see no end to the lines of inquiry uncoiling from the drama that played out on my microscope stage.

In pursuit of questions like these, nature study encourages a lively resonance between direct observation and secondhand learning, between organism or ecosystem and teacher or text. It also trains the curious observer to move supplely along an investigative spectrum ranging from rigorous research to imaginative speculation. In order to find what the world (to borrow Stafford's phrase) is trying to be, we have to come fresh to every observation. To study natural history requires us to set aside preconceptions, to be tutored by the world. Yet even as a student of nature learns to get out of the way, she must also bring her own intuitive sensibility to the project.

Geneticist Barbara McClintock, for example, credited her Nobel-winning discoveries to "a feeling for the organism." And science illustrator Jenny Keller points out, "If you're trying too hard to screen out the personal while you're drawing a bird, you're likely to screen out some things about the bird." Biologist and longtime birdwatcher Todd Newberry goes so far as to argue, in *The Ardent Birder*, that the art and science of watching birds, "for all its skill and paraphernalia, is at base an emotional enterprise." He published this book about his avocation in order to "share not only a skill and craft but also a state of mind—more, a state of heart, one akin to love."

For me, college botany became a gateway to the naturalist's path. Heartened by the surprising sense of excitement and satisfaction that I felt while sketching during lab sessions, I eventually took a couple of drawing classes and learned that instruction and practice could compensate for my lack of artistic talent. Sketching became a way of shedding preoccupation, of slowing down and inhabiting the moment. It remains one of my favorite tools for learning. In the decades since that initial encounter with a fern frond, I have spent countless hours with notebook and pen, being tutored by plants and bugs and birds, by deep forests and desert cliffs and rushing mountain streams, and by the people who have accompanied me there. As a teacher, I have enjoyed passing along this practice to children, teenagers, and adults.

And yet, as enlightening and compelling as informal natural history study may be, a nagging voice in my head sometimes asks whether it makes sense to continue indulging in this activity in a world that's falling down all around us. The question can be especially acute for sporadic amateur naturalists like me, whose discoveries are unlikely to save imperiled species or habitats, protect water supplies, or improve the practice of agriculture. Can we nature dilettantes really afford our dalliances? After all, when there is less and less of intact "nature" to observe, isn't it less important to *attend* than to *do something*?

But that's ultimately a fruitless question—and a false dichotomy. I believe we might as well ask whether there is still time for reverence, for gratitude and celebration, for music and education and art. The survival of viable ecosystems and the creation of sustainable human societies depend as urgently on the *attitudes* we cultivate as they do on our activism. Our children and grandchildren will never heal the world, or perhaps even feel compelled to try, if they fail to develop empathy and respect for the beauty and diversity, the complexity and interdependence, of all life. And they are not likely to get there without exposure to adults who model such appreciation. They need opportunities to meet nature head-on, whether in a biology lab or a school garden, along an urban lakeshore or on a mountaintop. They need encouragement to pay attention and to wonder.

I watch my university students at work making compost outside the gates of the teaching garden they built. Two of them grasp opposite sides of a large wire-mesh sieve framed with wooden boards and move the contraption vigorously back and forth between them. Their classmates shovel chunks of material onto the sieve from a dumpster-sized bin where food scraps, garden clippings, and manure have been keeping company with fungi and bacteria and bugs. In two months' time, the bin's contents have undergone a fecund transformation, surprising the novice composters in the group. Although these students have learned that bacteria produce heat in the process of breaking down organic matter, they're unprepared for their first contact with an active compost pile. Some reflexively pull their hands back, their eyes widening: the pile has more than doubled in temperature, rising to a sultry 140 degrees.

In the final compartment of the long composting bin, the corn husks and apple cores have disappeared. The wheelbarrow beneath the sieve fills with rich, moist granules, as dark and pleasantly aromatic as coffee grounds. The sifters run them through their hands with satisfaction; one woman brings a fistful to her nose and inhales. Another student wheels the compost through the garden gates and helps dig it into a new bed, where it will nourish the broccoli and eggplant and basil that will eventually grace the community dinner table.

These students are learning not only to pay respectful attention to natural cycles but also to work together and tend the earth with love and care in exchange for its gifts. In their bright eyes and easy movements, I see the pleasure of their growing erudition and community spirit, their fruitful intimacy with an ancient cycle that's as intriguing and essential and common as dirt.

Long belittled by modern academic scientists as a quaint, old-fashioned diversion, nature study should occupy the core of any twenty-first-century school curriculum. Rachel Carson anticipated this argument in 1952, when she accepted the Burroughs Medal for her book *The Sea Around Us*. "If we have ever regarded our interest in natural history as an escape from the realities of the modern world," she told those gathered at the award ceremony, "let us now reverse this attitude. For the mysteries of living things, and the birth and death of continents and seas, are among the great realities." In *Silent Spring*, Carson dramatized how military-industrial societies disregard and degrade those realities at our peril.

A highly educated woman I've known and liked since childhood is married to an architect who works on large commercial projects. This friend once told me that her husband had been hired to design a high-end shopping complex for a prosperous Midwestern suburb. When I asked her to describe the site where the project was to be built, she gazed at me blankly for a moment and then replied with a dismissive shrug: "Oh—it's just *empty land*." She didn't mean that the tract held no soil or water or topography or that no plants, birds, mammals, insects, or other organisms inhabited or interacted on it, only that the area had not yet been turned to direct human use. A global society increasingly peopled by humans who think this way—that is, the society in which we currently live—does not stand a robust chance of survival. Heedless of the intricate ecological webs that embrace and sustain us, we're destined to keep on tearing them apart.

Reclaiming nature study in schools and communities would be one fine way to follow the sage advice penned by Robert Hunter and sung by the Grateful Dead: "Wake up to find out that you are the eyes of the world." We are the eyes of the world. And we urgently need to see anew.

One of my dearest friends, a writer, artist, and former botanist who has found a midlife calling in religious leadership, recently observed that, like me, she was chastised as a young girl for her "oversensitive" nature. "I spent my whole childhood thinking that 'sensitive' was a bad word, like 'stupid' or 'ugly,'" she wrote to me, "and I was totally ashamed of that label. And then—miracle!—that childhood 'curse' turns out to be the gift that lets you love the world and all its wonderful, astonishing beings with a wide-open heart. Your heart. My heart. All of our hearts. Breaking all the time, and somehow still, if we are lucky and can stand it, going back out to love the world and heal it in the only ways we can."

I don't doubt that there are thousands of young people wandering around neighborhoods and schools at this moment, troubled by their own unique brands of "oversensitivity"—intellectually adrift, unable to find a match between their passions and the curricula on offer. I suggest that we provide them with microscopes and binoculars, a field guide and a fern, a notebook and a pen, a raised bed in which to plant some flowers and food. Let's give them a chance to find what the world is trying to be.

A Back Road Home

Ask yourself, and yourself alone, one question. Does this path have a heart? If it does, the path is good; if it doesn't, the path is of no use.

—Carlos Castaneda

My friend Jenny, a teacher of natural science illustration, often leads her classes on field sketching trips to the Monterey Bay Aquarium. On one such outing, the students dispersed as usual to draw the bright life in the pools and tanks, while Jenny detoured to the aquarium café to set up makeshift office hours. As she sat down at a table, her gaze lit on the saltshaker. It was nothing out of the ordinary, a clear jar with a perforated metal screw cap. Sunlight poured through the café windows, glinting on the white grains encased in glass and steel. Jenny reached for her sketchbook.

Absorbed in her work, she barely noticed the student who stopped by her table to stare. "Why are you drawing a saltshaker?" he asked. Jenny guessed what he was thinking: Why would she choose a mass-produced object, just like dozens she could have found closer to home? After all, the class had traveled fifty miles to sketch the neon-hued sea slugs, the shorebirds scuttling over sand, the levitating nautiluses in their painted shells. But none of that mattered to Jenny at the moment. The saltshaker had called out to her, that particular saltshaker in that specific shaft of light, and no other drawing she might have attempted just then could have proved more fruitful.

Jenny and I often return to the memory of this moment in our conversations. The saltshaker has become a touchstone for us, shorthand for the homing instinct we share. At a crossroads, torn about which way to go, each of us listens for the inner prompting that guided Jenny that day in the aquarium. Often difficult to hear, even harder to heed, this whisper of our deepest intuition can help guide us to good work. It turns our gaze toward beams of light that shine from unexpected sources. To be guided in this way, we often have to defy others' assumptions, sometimes our own.

Buddhists talk about the practice of "right livelihood," by which they mean, among other things, living mindfully and doing work that serves the world and causes no harm. I am no Buddhist scholar, and so I probably don't understand or embrace the concept of right livelihood in all its subtlety. But I like the idea, and I have respectfully extended it to apply to my own quest for what I might call a sacred vocation.

In this spirit, I take "right livelihood" to imply encouragement to cultivate spiritually satisfying work that arises out of passion, offers ample space to learn and grow, serves others, and suits a person's unique nature. I can think of few things that matter more. A girlfriend of mine used to say that the two keys to happiness were "true love and high adventure." Add right livelihood and you'd have a powerful recipe for a joyful life. Sadly, so many of us are tied up in the struggle for a mere living that this ideal may seem impossibly luxurious. As anthropologist Margaret Mead observed, in a perfect society, everyone would feel entitled to genuinely useful, gratifying work. We all need the experience of giving our best energies to the world just as acutely as we need freedom, kindness, and love.

Some gifted souls seem to slide effortlessly into their unique calling, into the passions and purposes of a lifetime. I turn wistful when I read about such people: the professional naturalist who terrorized his parents with his bedroom bug collection at the age of three; the prolific writer who drafted her first novel at twelve. I envy Jenny, who grew up with an artist mother, grandmother, and sister and who can't remember a time when she didn't draw.

My path has been more circuitous. No shining highway ever seemed to rise up before me. Instead, as my mother once pointed out after observing my meanderings from environmental advocacy to high school science teaching to medical reporting, I have "made myself up"—an enterprise that has its joys and its drawbacks. I take comfort in the wisdom of songwriter Kate Wolf, who sings in "Back Roads" that the most direct route to wherever we're headed may not be the best; she celebrates the unexpected gifts that come with the roundabout way. Along my personal back roads, I have learned a valuable lesson or two: for example, that careful analysis gets one only so far in matters of right livelihood. Faced with a difficult decision about the next step in my work life, I have always, ultimately, listened to the saltshaker voice. To put it another way, I have followed my heart. And while I have grieved the losses incurred in many of those heartfelt decisions, I have never regretted a one.

But what does it really mean, to "follow your heart"? For those of us who seem destined to struggle rather than soar into a life of good work, what useful truths can we discern beneath the surface of that facile phrase? And as we seek to give the best of ourselves to a world that we lament and love, what obstacles are we likely to meet along the path?

One summer, I read Barbara Kingsolver's novel *Animal Dreams*. Like other readers, I was bowled over by this tale of a search for joy and meaning in a difficult world. I recommended it to anyone who would listen. But even as I heard myself exclaiming how this was the most life-affirming novel I had encountered in years, I felt an aching gap between Kingsolver's triumphant narrative and my own unfinished story.

The following autumn, I attended a writers' workshop in southern Utah, where I studied with desert ethnobiologist Gary Nabhan. On the first night of the workshop, three dozen of us gathered after dinner in the cozy lodge at Pack Creek Ranch. A litter of half-wild kittens played just outside the window in the chilly fall dusk; inside, we sat bathed in the living room's lamp glow, nursing hot mugs of coffee and cocoa. When Gary spoke, he summed up his purpose as scientist, activist, and writer in a single sentence. "I try to help people cultivate sustainable relationships with the land," he said, "in the places where we work and live, in the places we love."

His words broke through the vague unease that had haunted me since I had read *Animal Dreams*. Sitting there in the crowded lodge, I began to understand why the novel had upset me so. The quest of Kingsolver's heroine, it seemed to me, was to find her proper home: not just geographically but emotionally, culturally, politically, spiritually. Codi Noline dared look for True Love, High Adventure, and Right Livelihood all in one place—Grace, Arizona, the home of her childhood. And even though she didn't arrive until the eleventh hour, she never settled for anything less than a true homecoming.

This was not my story. I had, in fact, settled. My teaching job and freelance writing brought me stimulation and some sense of usefulness; the Santa Cruz landscape embraced me; friendships nourished me. And yet that evening at Pack

Creek, I was forced to admit that I had given up on something vital.

As a teenager, I had imagined that the work I eventually found would help repair the heartbreaking rifts I saw around me—among people and also between people and the sacred places we were destroying. I had harbored vague yet sincere dreams of helping save my beloved coastal California homeland from the voracious development and shortsighted exploitation that were tearing it apart. But as an adult, sampling various disciplines and mastering none, I seemed to be skirting the edges of that adolescent hope. *Animal Dreams* had awakened me to a sobering truth: out of a lack of faith in myself, I had abandoned my own tentative vision of a deeply purposeful life. Now here was Gary, a great and brilliant soul, who not only dreamed his vision but also was living it. My admiration was matched by a fierce yearning to do the same.

Over the course of that four-day writing workshop, I reached a decision. Whatever it took, I would arrange for time off from my job, find the money to go back to school, and learn the naturalist's skills that would help me to become an effective champion of the lands I loved.

On my last night in Utah, I stayed at the home of an acquaintance in Moab. Casting about the living room for something to read, I found a small, spiral-bound collection of quotations published by the Hurricane Island Outward Bound School. Penciled onto the flyleaf was a quotation from *Animal Dreams*: "The very least you can do in your life," it said, "is to figure out what you hope for. And then the most you can do is live inside that hope. Not admire it from a distance but live right in it, under its roof." This time, Kingsolver's words bestowed not despair but support. With mounting determination, I found myself peering down the road toward the house of my hope, making plans to move in.

A year and a half later, I stood in an April snowstorm in northern Vermont, gazing toward New York State across twelve frozen miles of Lake Champlain. I had joined several graduate students on a birding trip. This was part of my three-day interview for a master's degree program for field naturalists, the most alluring option my search had turned up. Two years of intensive classroom work, interspersed with frequent day trips, followed by long weeks of fieldwork in New England, Alaska, Costa Rica—a dream come true. The program accepted only five new students each year, providing full scholarships and stipends. The aim was to teach people to be old-fashioned naturalists with contemporary knowledge, latter-day John Muirs who would be able to look at a landscape and understand the forces that had created it. Graduates of the program were expected to interpret the land to its human inhabitants, to midwife sustainable relationships between the two.

The program accepted me; I was ecstatic. By late spring, I was, mentally, on my way to Burlington, Vermont. I sent notices for a friend to post in the local food co-op, advertising for a place to live. I heard from an art professor who was interested in sharing her home with me. She lived in a two-bedroom house with a garden on an island on the lake, twenty minutes' drive from campus. We liked each other over the phone. I would live with her in the fall, and when she went on sabbatical in the spring, I would have the house to myself for the same low rent. I hoped a real home with a working adult might offset the jarring transition from professional life to the potentially infantilizing role of graduate student. A small house in the country with lots of privacy seemed exactly right.

But when I called four or five future teachers and senior classmates with this news, they were skeptical. Not a good idea, they warned. Forget the house on the island. You'll be so busy in this program, you'll want an apartment next door to campus, where you can crash for the odd twenty minutes between commitments. You'll be heading into the field at six in the morning and back to campus in the late afternoon for classes, up late for evening lectures, library research, paper writing, number crunching. You'll be lucky to get a decent night's sleep, to remember to eat, to find time for anything other than schoolwork. And if you really care about having a garden, this is probably not the right program for you.

I recalled a scene during my on-site interview: between meetings with faculty members, I rested briefly in the cramped, chaotically messy room housing the graduate students' study carrels. One student chatted with another while her right hand pecked at a computer keyboard; in her left, she held an entire head of cabbage, gnawing hungrily at it between sentences. I got the feeling she hadn't eaten a real meal in quite some time.

One student I especially liked poured out her frustration over the phone. Describing a typical field trip, she said, "There we'd be on the shoulder of a mountain on a gorgeous New England fall day, the air crisp and the trees aflame with color—and we'd be totally stressing ourselves out. We'd be so hurried and uptight about collecting our data, doing it right, making sense out of it, that it seemed to me we would forget what had brought us into the field in the first place. I got branded as the token touchy-feely flake because I was always the one to ask, 'Doesn't anybody want to stop for fifteen minutes and just see where we are on this mountain?' Nobody seemed to get what I was talking about."

To stop and see where we were on the mountain was what I wanted more than anything else. For all its gifts, this graduate program suddenly seemed to have come at the wrong time in my life. Certainly it could teach me a great deal and much that I wanted desperately to learn. Yet I balked at the hoops I would have to jump through on the way. I was willing to work hard, but I didn't have it in me to turn myself into a caffeinated wreck or repress my emotional and artistic inclinations in order to become a better naturalist.

Turning down this opportunity seemed an enormous risk: in doing so, I might make the mistake of a lifetime. When I sought help with my dilemma from friends and colleagues, some reinforced my fears. They reminded me of the practical benefits of a master's degree and urged me to put up with the program's frenetic demands for two years in order to reap its rich benefits. Their advice made logical sense, but it failed to pacify my troubled spirit.

When resolution finally dawned, it began with a series of dreams that featured a female mountain lion. On each of several nights, this silent cat, emanating calm power, urged me to trust my instincts. A month later, still wrestling with my decision, I was back in Utah—this time to teach a writing and drawing workshop with Jenny. Perusing the library shelves at the field school sponsoring our class, I picked up a book of Native American wisdom about animal totems. I flipped it open at random to the following passage: "If Mountain Lion has come to you in dreams, it is a time to stand on your convictions and lead yourself where your heart takes you."

I returned to California and withdrew from the graduate program. I chose instead to take an independent year, live off my savings and income from freelance writing, and explore my home territory. I walked around my neighborhood, took note of what lived and grew there, watched otters play and pelicans dive in the nearby harbor, attended to subtle changes in the seasons and in my own state of mind. I wrote and researched nearly every day. I traveled and taught outdoor writing workshops. I took a sketching class from Jenny and learned to make visual as well as verbal records of my experiences in the field. In this fashion, I did acquire a bit of natural history knowledge—not through disciplined or systematic study but by observing closely and teaching myself to ask questions about what I noticed.

I can't say that I ever fully resolved the longings that emerged at the Pack Creek writing workshop. But neither do I regret the grad school decision. I felt increasingly expansive and joyful over the course of my independent year. Somehow, even though I haven't become the skilled naturalist I so hoped to be by now, my work is edging closer to right livelihood.

I have also begun to see with more forgiving eyes the crazy quilt of abilities and activities that make up my vocational history. At first glance, my peripatetic work life may not appear as focused or productive as the careers of my mentors and admired colleagues. But as I persevere on the path I've chosen, the patterns and meanings of my particular right livelihood are coming into focus. Can I say that I now can give more to the world because of my year of exploration— my year "on," as I came to call it? I don't know for certain. But I take courage from Mary Oliver's poem "Wild Geese," in which she writes, "You do not have to be good... You only have to let the soft animal of your body love what it loves." Perhaps to do what we love most *is* to do well by the world. Maybe it helps not to worry so much about whether we are doing the exact right thing, the best most responsible most impressive thing, and instead to trust that our work will be of use if it brings joy.

I don't mean that we should sell ourselves short or be cavalier about our potential or responsibilities. But I do think that, misled by self-critical and self-punishing voices, one can easily misconstrue one's calling. In thinking we need to Change the World, we may miss opportunities to perform the small yet profound acts of which we're truly capable.

For women, the effort to create a sacred vocation may entail a unique element of challenge. Certainly, men in this society have their own struggles in the search for meaningful work—struggles rooted, for example, in expectations that males should equip themselves as providers before considering their own creative passions. Yet the men I admire—at least those who grew up with some resources and encouragement—seem to proceed from a strong sense of entitlement to right livelihood. They tend to plunge in, trusting their enthusiasms. On the other hand, many of the women I know, including those who are unquestionably talented, battle an insidious lack of confidence in their own value as makers and doers.

Perhaps this is because so many of us feel so strongly about the prime importance of winning and bestowing love, which we may have been led to think means putting others' comfort before our own creative drive. For women like me, lucky enough to grow up in a loving, middle-class family and to benefit from a university education, these voices are oddly mingled with encouragement to do well and make a difference in the world of work. The result is a debilitating tension between accelerator and brake, an attenuated trust in our own instincts.

Even as I write this essay, I hear an imagined reader dismissing it as self-indulgent, irrelevant. Why waste column inches agonizing on paper, nags this critical voice, when I could and should just be *out* there, like dozens of male scientist-writers, doing the work, writing about What Matters, saving the world?

But for me, this *is* the work, even if it's only a saltshaker. If it calls, there's something in it of value that I must attend to. I keep a scrap from Annie Dillard's *The Writing Life* plastered to the wall beside my desk: "Why do you never find anything written about that idiosyncratic thought you avert to, about your fascination with something no one else understands? Because it is up to you." If self-doubt is part of my internal landscape, then rather than comparing myself with others and inwardly competing with their accomplishments, I must acknowledge my particular struggle, tell its stories— even as I attempt to move through and past my limitations. I have to hope that, rendered skillfully, honest words about my own hard lessons will constitute an offering that may benefit somebody else.

It helps to remember that we can't ever fully know the impact of our actions. My friend Ginger, a ranger and naturalist, used to lead snowshoe walks at Yosemite's Badger Pass each winter and work summers in Tuolumne Meadows. One summer season, out for a jog on her afternoon off, she heard someone call her name. It was a participant from one of her winter programs several years before. To Ginger's utter surprise, the woman recognized her without any difficulty and insisted on thanking her for the long-ago walk.

"I was never a very outdoorsy person," she said. "When you were introducing that snowshoe walk near the Badger Pass lodge, it started to snow. I watched the flakes begin to accumulate on your Smokey-the-Bear hat, and I thought for sure you were going to cancel the walk. I was amazed when you seemed to think nothing of the weather and turned to lead us off into the woods.

"That moment changed me somehow. I realized, watching you take that snowstorm completely in stride—even enjoy it—that maybe I didn't have to be so afraid."

Ginger had only been acting naturally, doing her job, yet this alone had provided an epiphany. At the time, she had no idea what she'd accomplished—just as Gary Nabhan couldn't know how his public words would serve as the catalyst for a change in my life. Ginger's story reminds me that we often serve others best simply by honoring what we care about most. "To find our calling," wrote theologian Frederick Buechner, "is to find the intersection between our own deep gladness and the world's deep hunger."

During the Great Depression of the 1930s, landscape photographer Ansel Adams took considerable criticism for favoring images of the natural world over documentation of the era's rampant poverty, unemployment, and other social ills. In 1943, Adams did, in fact, produce a powerful photo essay about the Japanese American relocation camp at Manzanar, but for the most part, he felt compelled to train his lens on wilderness. In a 1935 letter to his friend Dorothea Lange, he wrote, "I think it is just as important to bring to people the evidence of the beauty of the world of nature and of man as it is to give them a document of ugliness, squalor and despair." Adams insisted on following his deepest promptings. He couldn't have known that his images of mountains, forests, rivers, and deserts would end up helping save the wilderness he loved.

Finding Carlos Castaneda's "path with heart" is both a solitary and a social process. As he says, you do ultimately have to ask "yourself, and yourself alone," which way to go. But that's not the whole story, for we often play an essential role in each other's journeys. I cannot recall any of the watershed decisions in my life without remembering the books that inspired me and the friends and colleagues who helped by listening, reflecting me back to myself, offering their wisdom and affirming their trust in my choices.

Moreover, vocation itself depends upon community. Even the maverick artists among us create meaningful work in a social context. I remember the parachute we played with in sixth-grade gym class. The PE and dance teacher helped us spread the expanse of white nylon over the blond wood floor of our high-ceilinged auditorium, then had us squat around it—a couple dozen kids spaced evenly in a circle, each hanging onto the edge of that great gossamer cloth. At her signal, we'd rise quickly and run inward to stand, clutching the edge of the parachute in our hands while we raised our arms in unison. The air would rush in beneath and the parachute would billow up over our heads, an exultant dome. Briefly, it seemed that the upward momentum would continue pulling the chute toward the ceiling, taking us with it. Then the tension on our upstretched arms would ease, the chute would gradually collapse and float to the floor, and we would back up and stoop to begin again.

My classmates and I relied on a circle of comrades to give shape to our parachute. We were rooted in place yet in motion together. In order to take flight, a life of good work requires not only the air to buoy it but the hands to hold it in place. "No strings, no flight," mused the writer William Least Heat Moon as he passed a couple of boys flying kites along one of the back roads of North America. Making ourselves up requires a skillful combination of independence and connection.

The other day I watched my artist friend Jenny teach my writing students. They were keeping journals, and I had invited her to show them how writing complements the drawings in her own notebooks. In her body language and her voice, I sensed the care she had invested in preparing for this class. In the light shining from her eyes, I picked up reflections from that old aquarium saltshaker. I knew that Jenny has become a teacher not by straining outward toward professional achievement but by tapping her own heart's wisdom. In my own quest for a life of good work, I return to this lesson again and again.

Lessons from the Sharp End of the Pen:
Responding Respectfully to Student Writing

Try again. Fail again. Fail better.

—Samuel Beckett

When I was an undergraduate at Harvard in the 1970s, I enrolled in a course called "Education, Learning, and Theories and Practice of Teaching." I no longer remember the particulars of the course's term-paper prompt, but I do recall with excruciating vividness the dismissive, disparaging quality of the comments my instructor scribbled in the margins of my essay. Many years later, that professor's lacerating tone still haunts me—as a reminder of the power that we teachers can wield, for better or worse, with our pens.

My essay presented a critique of American public high school education. I drew my ideas from my own school experiences, from the theories of John Dewey and Jerome Bruner, and from the writings of my favorite educational reformers at the time: Kozol, Kohl, Holt, Illich, Dennison, Ashton-Warner.

As with most of my college papers, I spent more time agonizing helplessly over this one than actually writing it, and the professor's criticisms were probably accurate. I'm sure my composition lacked coherence and clout. It may have bristled with the naive generalities and righteous indignation that colored my early attempts at social criticism. I had not yet learned to integrate the emotions that animated my writing with the reasoning that might have steadied it. Also, although I had inherited my parents' love of language, I had almost zero rhetorical training. I'd benefited from a couple of good high school English classes and I'd aced the college aptitude tests, yet I'd never learned how to compose an extended critical analysis or sustain a complex argument. And I knew few practical techniques for drafting, organizing, or revising an academic essay. All of these shortcomings must have shown up in my paper.

Even so, I did care fervently about what I was trying to say, and I'm pretty sure that my words reflected that passion. I wanted to write persuasively. But I needed help—help that my instructor might have given had he approached his comments differently. Besides pointing out the limitations of my research and my reasoning, he might have affirmed my impulse to articulate fledgling insights, encouraging me to nurture them further. Rather than expressing impatience with my paper's inadequacies, he might have suggested some steps I could take to transcend its limitations. In short, he might have responded to my essay as a live work in progress rather than a fixed portrait of my failures.

The fact that this instructor—and others like him—did not comment on my papers as I might have wished doesn't necessarily reflect badly on his teaching. The university's educational system saddled him with significant limitations. For one, he was required to give me a letter grade. Since his comments had to justify that grade, they had to serve, at least in part, as a judgment of the quality of my work—a very different sort of comment from the kind that cultivates a constructive student-teacher dialogue. As I've since learned, it's difficult, if not impossible, to compose paper comments that establish or reinforce a grade while simultaneously helping a student grow as a thinker and writer.

Furthermore, this instructor may have considered it beyond his purview to help me write a good paper. He was, after all, an education professor, not a composition teacher. His job was to determine how well I had assimilated the course material, to evaluate the quality of my ideas, and to assess the originality and effectiveness of my argument. He was not supposed to teach me to write.

This view may seem sensible. It is certainly common among instructors outside of writing programs. But I believe it rests on a significant misunderstanding about how people learn. Usually, we come to understand a new concept while we write about it—by writing about it. And we hone our writing skills in the process of learning to think. It's in the midst of this process that we most need a teacher's help and can best make use of it.

An inferior essay may be unsatisfactory in part because of verbal and rhetorical problems—but frequently the flaws stem from the writer's difficulties thinking effectively in an unfamiliar discipline. To remedy what ails a piece of writing, a student may need less to be tutored in correct syntax or formal essay structure than to be directed toward relevant texts, shown where her thinking has gone astray, or taught what constitutes a useful question in the field and why. She may simply need affirmation for finding the trailhead herself and a gentle push to get her moving.

I had one teacher in college—Betty Farrell, the leader of my sophomore tutorial in sociology—who saw this kind of interaction as part of her charge. I credit her with keeping me in school. She helped me to believe that I had a head on my shoulders, and she showed me how to use it. She would regularly type one or two single-spaced pages of impressions in response to each student's paper. She encouraged us to revise our essays, or at least to see each one as a stepping-stone rather than a finished product. In her comments—sometimes more extensive than the essays to which they were appended—she paraphrased our assertions, explored implications, proposed counterarguments, offered new perspectives, and recommended texts for us to consult.

Betty responded seriously to her students' ideas—sometimes taking issue but always in service of prodding our thinking further, and always in such a warmly encouraging tone that I felt inspired rather than demoralized, engaged rather than embattled. Without abnegating her role as our teacher, she modeled a generous and respectful style of collegial interaction. She conveyed the belief that she had something useful to learn from each of us. She was genuinely interested in what we had to say and how we might say more or say it better. When we fell short of what she believed to be our own capacities, she let us know, but without judging. She seemed to see clearly into the best thinker in each of us—and that's what she elicited.

A big part of what teachers and tutors can do for students, then, is to help them understand not only that a draft is unsatisfactory but also what its flaws suggest about the next step in the student's learning. Unlike exams, papers are not simply performances that demonstrate the scope of the student's knowledge to date. They are live documents whose value lies largely in their potential for revision or discussion. The tradition of assigning a final, one-draft term paper may be time-honored, but pedagogically, it's counterproductive. My education professor's ability to help me was hampered not only by his obligation to grade my essay but also by his perspective within the paradigm of paper as finished product.

But while my instructor's response to my paper may have been shaped by institutional constraints, it need not so stridently have stifled my momentum as a learner. The most troublesome aspect of his comments, for me as a student, was their exasperated tone. To convey a disdainful attitude in responding to student papers can short-circuit the learning process—painfully and unnecessarily.

I can certainly imagine why my prof's comments might have bristled with annoyance. To him, my paper's shortcomings probably suggested laziness, cluelessness, poor preparation, failure to fulfill the assignment's expectations. Nevertheless, in using the margins of my essay to vent his frustration, he did us both a disservice: he framed my mistakes as emblems of failure rather than as opportunities for further learning.

Had it occurred to this instructor to do so, he might, with little extra effort, have transformed his terminal judgments into open-ended exhortation. Take, for example, this statement: "No—you are misrepresenting the author here." Reading sentences like this scrawled in the margins of my returned papers as a college student, I couldn't help but infer that I'd failed at an important task—failed to fully understand the text with which I had tried to engage, failed to paraphrase its message accurately. I felt stupid: the text represented an authoritative voice; I was a mediocre novice scholar lacking the intellectual acuity required to grasp its message. And I felt accused of dishonesty; I had twisted the source text, if unwittingly, in order to bolster my own argument.

What if, instead, the teacher had written, "Go back and reread the passage you're referring to here. Where does your paraphrase depart from the writer's actual message? Would it be helpful to explore the reasons why you interpreted it as you did?" Like the original comment, this one points out my error—but in language that implies an assumption that I am both interested in and capable of learning from that error and moving beyond it. It also opens up the possibility that fruitful discoveries might be made inside the gap between my original representation of the source text and a more accurate second reading.

Other judgmental marginalia could be similarly revised. "This is a serious oversimplification" might become "Can you imagine a more complicated, more accurate way of understanding and presenting this problem?" Likewise, "Not everybody would agree with you here" might be rephrased as "Okay, but how might somebody argue who disagrees with you, and how would you respond?"

Each of these comments has a subtext. The first in each pair positions the instructor as a carrier—though not necessarily a conveyer—of correct knowledge and astute insight, one whose job it is to assess how the student's effort measures up. Every one of these marginalia makes clear that the writer has failed at some task, but it fails to encourage or equip her to go beyond that failure. The revised comment, on the other hand, puts the instructor in the role of both capable critic and interested reader, and it casts the student as both an apprentice and an independent agent of her own learning. It not only points out a problem but also points to the next step, helping the student see what's entailed in more resourceful writing.

Not intentionally but perhaps not surprisingly, each rewritten comment takes an interrogative form. Whereas declarative sentences all too easily convey judgment and preempt further exchange, questions can suggest new directions and open up dialogue. Moving from one voice to the other shifts the essential premise of the teacher-student enterprise from performance assessment to constructive collaboration.

Now that I am the teacher wielding the pen, my vivid recall of this decades-old incident instructs me about the potential impact of my own responses to student writing. In particular, it reminds me that the spirit in which I deliver my comments matters. I don't presume that all or even most of my students are profoundly affected one way or another by what I write in their margins. But I do believe that once in a while, my comments make a memorable impression, whether constructive or destructive. Since I never know when that moment might arise, I set myself a goal of approaching each student's paper with as much respect as I can muster.

This means not that I coddle or patronize but that I try not to disparage or dismiss. I frequently imagine myself on the receiving end of my own comments. If a student's voice in a paper strikes me as exasperatingly simplistic or strident, I remind myself how I probably came across to my own beleaguered professors years ago and how hard I was trying at the time regardless of the impression I may have conveyed. I imagine the writer of each paper as receptive to my criticisms, suggestions, and encouragement—an exercise aided when possible by personal contact with my students during class time and office hours. I raise questions; I point to alternative directions or necessary work left undone. When students seem hardly to have tried, I reflect that impression back to them. But I always aim to communicate my interest in the process that brought them to their written work as it currently stands, and my belief in the subsequent steps that can move it further along.

I sometimes fall dismayingly short of my own ideals. When I'm trying to turn around a pile of fifty papers—between teaching and preparing classes, finishing up last quarter's narrative evaluations, attending to administrative work, attempting to get to my own writing, and living the rest of my life—the point of my pen may get sharper or blunter than I'd like. Sometimes, when the stacks of papers become burdensome and my hand aches at the thought of another long comment-writing session, I substitute email exchanges or office conferences for written responses, in order to sustain my own enthusiasm.

But whatever the medium, and no matter how brief, I try to make the message as respectful as possible. Years from now, when my former students bend to a writing task, I imagine that some will occasionally hear an echo of my voice. Rather than haunting their efforts, I hope it cheers them on.

Sailing into Now

For the second year in a row, a late July morning finds me on the southwestern shore of Lake Superior, gathering with my students in a nature writing workshop called Wordscapes. We sprawl along the lakeside dock in the resort village of Bayfield, Wisconsin, with our collective mountain of gear and our private thoughts. We're waiting for the chartered sailboat that will take us to Stockton Island, part of the Apostle chain, where for five days we'll camp and hike, swim and write.

It's a bright, scrubbed morning with a benign breeze, but I'm glum. Over the past couple of days my usually high spirits have plummeted, and I'm feeling sunken, stymied, a bad fit in my own skin. Even the teaching adventure on which I am about to embark looms like a series of daunting chores. Aware that the students have their own uncertainties and discomforts and eager to serve as the attentive instructor they deserve, I try to tuck my personal misery away. Ashamed as I am to admit it even to myself, though, the one pleasure I'm truly looking forward to is greeting my lover back home at the far end of the week.

I hate feeling so detached, so pinched off from happiness that ought to be within reach. There's nothing specific wrong; I'm just mildly, inexplicably down, disconnected from the life going on in and around me. Maybe it's hormones. Whatever the cause, when this mood hits, there are only a few remedies I know to try: writing, for example, and walking, and the grace of good company. Such tonics can help bring me back to what is happening here and now. And so what I'm hoping to offer my students on the island over the next several days is the same thing I need for myself: a way into the arms of the present.

Our charter captain finally motors into view, throwing out fenders and snugging his 36-foot boat along the dock. We form a bucket brigade to stow our endless stream of belongings belowdecks. The vessel's name is *Tranquility*, which I take to be a good sign until the captain, Rick, informs us that her head is clogged and her gauges don't work.

As we untie from the dock and motor out of the marina, I remember last year's Wordscapes: my first visit to the Apostle Islands and my first sailing trip as more than just a passenger—not that I'd realized I'd be doing any crewing. Without warning, Rick threaded a line through a grommet in the corner of a sail, tossed this bit of rigging at me, told me to secure it with a bowline, and disappeared. I didn't know a bowline from a bowtie. As I fumbled with canvas and nylon, I imagined my bungled knot sending the sail flapping into the lake. I spent the rest of that trip avoiding Rick's gaze, hoping he wouldn't ask for any further help.

This year, though, things go better. I notice the integrity and kindness that underlie Rick's chain-smoking bravado, and I muster some boldness of my own. Maybe I actually *can* tie a knot, haul up a sail, or even take the helm. I ply Rick with questions, trying to match boats and rigs to the terms I've heard: sloops and ketches, schooners and yawls; wherries, dories, dinghies, catboats. I glean the difference between Marconi rigs and gaff rigs, sheets and halyards; I sort out headsail and mainsail, genny and jib. I'm learning the sailors' poetry: nautical wordscapes. Even so, I manage to make a fool of myself once again. Trying to pump a cupful of water in the galley, I raise and lower the apparently pump-like faucet arrangement to no avail, until a couple of snickering companions show me the foot pedal on the floor beneath the basin.

After three and a half hours on the lake, we tie up at Stockton Island's Presque Isle Bay dock, extract our luggage, and say goodbye to Rick. He will send another captain for us on Tuesday. We hoof our supplies and equipment up the forested half-mile path to our lake-view campsite, four luggage-laden trips apiece. By the time we've pitched our tents and fetched our water, I know I'm not the only grumpy camper.

That night, one of the students confides in me that she's put her foot in her mouth during some bit of conversation earlier that day; the sting of it lingers. I listen and commiserate and encourage her to let the discomfort go. I invoke a favorite Emerson quotation: "Finish each day and be done with it. You have done what you could. Some blunders and absurdities no doubt crept in; forget them as soon as you can. Tomorrow is a new day. Begin it well and serenely, and with too high a spirit to be encumbered with your old nonsense." Still smarting from my own trivial gaffe with the water pump, I'm struck by the relative ease with which I urge self-forgiveness on another.

The next morning I open my eyes to the call of a loon—*hoohooHEEHEEhoo, hoohooHEEHEEhoo*—and the sight of a rainbow out my tent door. The colors arc over the tree-furred mainland on the western horizon, beyond a smooth and beckoning lake. Walt appears with a brown plastic cup full of hot coffee brewed from Mary's generous stash of organic French roast. "Madame," he intones, bowing ceremoniously outside the screen door, "would you like your coffee in bed this morning?"

Sunning together on the lee side of the island, the students and I work on a writing exercise. I have asked each of them to choose an emotion to convey through a series of brief sensory vignettes: just concrete detail, no abstractions. Each writer reads the resulting poem aloud, and we all note the way they call up strong feelings without naming them. I've written

> A fly in honey; a leg-trapped dog
> Locked brakes, rusted bolts
> A thicket of thorns that catch and hold . . .

But as the days unfold, something does begin to come loose. At the campfire one night, I listen while Claudia reads poems she has written in memory of the grandmother she lost, a prolific gardener and cook whose death still stirs Claudia—and now us—to tears. I laugh at Sheila's spontaneous dramatic improvs, a one-woman miniseries with proliferating characters and thickening plots. I groan at Walt's and Eric's bartender jokes, the after-dinner humor growing raunchier by the day. I admire Mary's pen-and-ink sketches. I wash off hot-weather grime in the lake's clean swells, and some of my bleakness seems to fall away with the sweat and dirt.

One overcast morning, while the students are occupied with an assignment, I spend several hours poking along the sandy beach of the leeward shore and then back to camp through forest and bog. The sky is packed with gray-green cotton; red-tinged sand matches my summer skin. Rigging on a lone anchored sailboat clangs softly from the bay. Dressed comfortably in a bathing suit and shorts, I walk ankle-deep in warm water over rippled sand, the absence of sticky salt a constant surprise. I'm accustomed to the ocean beach near my house, two thousand miles from here; a freshwater lake as big as the sea is a wonder to me. I'm caressed by the fresh but muted air of this place—biting flies the only stitch of insult in the silken fabric of the day.

In the forest, sensations streak toward me like the opening screen in a Star Wars movie. A moth the size of an eye patch darts at my face. White birch and aspen trunks stripe the evergreen darkness. Berries shine out from the foliage: stoplight-red dogwood, waxy ripe blueberries, purple Juneberries, indigo blue-bead lilies, half-hidden crimson wintergreen tucked drooping under low leaves. My notebook is constantly in my hand, my pen traveling easily. I'm pumping life onto the page the way a new butterfly pumps it into her wings.

On our last night in camp, I get up to pee around midnight and see the Milky Way painted thickly from zenith to horizon, as if I were standing inside a black billiard ball with a white stripe. In the morning, I wake to the tick of rain on my tent. We pack and haul our gear to the dock under a barrage of thundercracks.

But weather moves fast in northern Wisconsin, and the sky clears for our late-morning journey back to Bayfield. John, our captain on the return leg, continues my nautical education. We're under sail all the way home, and I stand at the *Tranquility's* helm, gripping the binnacle or bracing against the stern pulpit. I get the hang of keeping the flapping blue telltales, little wind flags, at a forty-five-degree angle to our line of travel, aiming the bow toward a point of land up ahead. We skim along with full sails, sometimes heeling over so far I can practically touch the lake. Playing the wheel left and right to keep our heading, I hold the wind in my hands. I don't even know I'm grinning until someone's camera points at me from the cabin door and I realize I've lost all self-consciousness, flying through the day under blue sky and just feeling mindlessly happy.

At some point I will end up back in that drearier place. But this outing has reminded me that even in the dark moments, I have to plant myself right here on deck, breathing dank air if that's what the breeze carries my way. With a bit of luck, if I let in the goodwill of others and the balm of lake and forest, the wind will eventually shift.

A Great Excuse to Stare

Student: "How do you draw grass?"
Jenny: "You need to ask the grass. Otherwise you miss out on all the things grass is."

I once overheard a couple of college students poring over a sketchbook that one of them had pulled out of her backpack. "Wow, that's *beautiful*," exclaimed the artist's friend. "Look at those feathers! . . . And that one of the woman and her dog is AMAZING. You're so GOOD!" Then, with a defeated sigh: "I wish I could do what you do. I can't even draw a stick figure."

"Oh, *any*body can learn to draw. I really believe that now," came the second voice, confident and reassuring. I thought I knew what she would say next—and sure enough: "You just have to have the right teacher. Like Jenny."

My friend Jenny Keller is a breathtaking artist and an award-winning teacher of science illustration. Over the decades of our friendship, I have audited her classes, taught alongside her in the field, and enjoyed countless conversations about our respective crafts. She has taught me many things—most importantly that *seeing*, in the deepest sense, is more than a technical challenge; it's an ethical stance, a way of relating to the world. And it can be taught. Take a class from Jenny or listen to her talk about her work and you find yourself in the presence of a spiritual guide.

Once, in a rust-and-jade river canyon in southern Utah, Jenny and I were sitting side by side bent over our notebooks when suddenly she grinned over at me midsketch and declared, "That's the main reason I love to draw: It's a great excuse to *stare* at things!"

"That's what artists do," she said a short while later to the students in the writing and drawing workshop we were jointly leading. "It's nothing tricky. They force themselves to *look*." But, said a student, there's so much to see. How do you know what to draw? "The world is gigantic," Jenny acknowledged. "You have to narrow it down to what matters at the moment. Choose a subject that beckons to you: a shell, a person, a landscape, whatever. You don't have to think you can draw it. If it interests you, it's important. That interest will take you through the tough spots. What motivates me to finish a drawing is intensely *wanting* the thing I'm going to end up with. Artists see the world and snag it and make it their own."

Jenny always balances her exhortations with explicit instruction. "First of all, let me just say that drawing is a learnable skill," she said that day on the river. "You all have the manual dexterity it takes to draw; the trick is training your hand and eye to work together." She invoked a story about the time she broke her right arm and learned, in just a few days, to draw with her left: "Coordination is a little part of it, but *seeing* is everything."

I mulled over my own experiences with drawing—an activity at which I feel continually humbled. For me, "seeing" has come to mean going into the back yard with a sketchbook and a pen, sitting down in front of a clematis blossom, and letting the flower teach me. On a good day, I can keep my attention on the plant itself, ignoring concerns about making a "good" picture. At those times, the process of looking and drawing loosens my cramped spirit, opens my pores, wakes me up. I come away from my sketching session tingling, as after a run. It is this open, attentive stance that imbues drawing with meaning and delight.

"Usually what stalls us in drawing is getting critical," Jenny observed. "In blind contour"—a sketching practice in which the artist looks only at the object being drawn, not at the drawing—"you *can't* decide what looks good or bad. In fact, the finished drawing doesn't really matter. Properly done contour drawings end up looking wild, anyway, kind of like possessed steel wool. What *does* matter is the process— learning to move your eyes and hand at the same slow pace. The drawing you'll be left with is just a by-product, but you will see in it parts of the personality of your subject.

"Another thing that can cause problems in drawing is unconsciously relying on memory. What we've memorized before can actually get in the way of what we see now. But when you do a contour drawing and have to focus so intently on your subject, preconceived ideas of what something should look like just can't get in the way. You draw what you see, not what you think you know. Even though the proportions or placement may be distorted, the personality will be there."

A student asked Jenny about the rules of composition. By way of introduction, she replied, "Talking about composition is a bit like talking about how to drive a car. Learning about all those controls can make you lose your natural grace for a while. But eventually it all becomes like second nature. Just so with drawing. You already have a natural, perfect sense of composition. Don't let what I tell you freeze you up. Take it in, then forget about it."

One warm, breezy October morning by the shores of Monterey Bay, I took part in a field trip Jenny led to get students drawing trees. We could hear sea lions barking, prop planes buzzing overhead, surf washing against the cliff a quarter mile from our sketching spot. In spite of the lovely day, I found myself becoming more and more miserable as I struggled to draw a Monterey cypress. It came out stiff and graceless. When Jenny walked over to see how I was doing, my frustration poured out.

"You are in a class, after all," she reminded me. "This is your place to make mistakes and do experiments. You need to not be so invested in the outcome, but present and sincere in your actions in this moment. Allow your curiosity, rather than a feeling of obligation, to rise and hold you focused. If you're stuck, you need to keep trying."

As my mood cleared, Jenny borrowed my pencil and showed me wedge-shaped strokes and how to build them up to suggest clumps of foliage. She pulled a quotation from her bountiful repertoire, this one from Andre Gide's journals: "The thing I am most aware of is my limits. And this is natural, for I never, or almost never, occupy the middle of my cage; my whole being surges toward the bars."

"Sometimes when you're having the most trouble," she said, "it's because you're standing at the border of your safe territory and you're trying to expand it. Don't think there's something wrong just because it's a struggle. That's how it ought to be when you're learning at the edge."

Of course, I thought. As a teacher and a writer, I know this; as an art student, I have to be reminded. To grow beyond the skin we're wearing now requires stretching it to the breaking point—and feeling, for a time, its painful constriction. We sometimes get bogged down at this stage, woefully aware of our limitations. The mistake is thinking that we're stuck with the tattered membrane that's gradually giving way—and missing the glint of supple new skin emerging underneath.

When students bring me new drafts of writing, their moods hovering between frustrated disappointment and tentative pride, part of my job is to show them the new powers breaking through here and there on the page.

After Jenny helped me recover my beginner's faith, as I continued sitting in on her class, I noted the return of my old tendency to look for the "good" and "bad" performances in the group—to judge on the basis of some quality of line or composition whether each of my fellow student-artists "had it" or didn't. I evaluated my own work with equal harshness and ended up careening between smug self-approval and disconsolate self-reprobation. I tried with incomplete success to make a mantra of Annie Dillard's advice: "The feeling that the work is magnificent, and the feeling that it is abominable, are both mosquitoes to be repelled, ignored, or killed, but not indulged."

Jenny anticipated the potential of competition and envy to poison the class atmosphere. Before the first "critique," when all of the students were to post our finished drawings on the wall for commentary, she headed us off at the pass. "Whether you feel intimidated or inspired by someone else's good work is your choice," she said. "You can ask the creator of something you admire how they did it. Learn from them."

I did come to see that every student had a touch, an approach, a discovery to offer. I also renewed my belief in everyone's ability, including my own, to learn and improve. Jenny's manner in presenting our work to each other underscored this fact. She pointed out and admired the successes she saw in each sketch, even as she offered suggestions for refinement. I began to feel truly part of a group—to feel the rich weave of individual strengths enhancing and reinforcing each other.

Naturalist and teacher Ken Norris, one of Jenny's mentors during her undergraduate years at UC Santa Cruz, had a favorite exclamation for the beginning of any journey—whether an expedition to Baja in a broken-down school bus or a jaunt to the hardware store in the family jalopy. "We're off on the greatest adventure of our lives!" he'd crow, and everyone aboard felt his ebullience. In the same spirit, Jenny prepares to teach a class as if it is to be a celebration of the most wonderful aspects of life on that day. Another drawing instructor with whom I once studied had a habitual way of talking about the tools of our craft: "Okay, take out your weapons," he'd exhort us. Jenny calls them "toys." As both teacher and artist, she takes an infectious pleasure in her work. No matter what their mood at the beginning of her classes, students usually walk out in high spirits.

Even so, Jenny says, "in spite of managing somehow to become a teacher, I think of myself as a shy person." This might surprise her students, with whom her warm enthusiasm makes her seem anything but reticent. Like many creative people, she has both a public and an intensely private side. She often craves solitude—as an antidote to the extreme social outwardness of teaching and as a necessary condition for nourishing her own work. One day she told me, "Sometimes I think I'm only really myself when I'm drawing." She can happily spend days alone with an art project. Yet even during those inward moments, she is likely to reach out. Often, her favorite work is inspired by the desire to bestow a gift. "The most wonderful times I've had drawing were when I was creating something for a friend," she says. "Every brush stroke is like some softly spoken word. And it's produced some of my best drawings."

Not just when she's alone at her drawing table but also on field trips with students, hikes with friends, and everyday errands, Jenny pulls out her sketchbook at the drop of a hat. "Rarely am I conscious of the moment of *starting* a drawing," she says. "It's so enticing that it pulls you in before you know it. Beginning a drawing, I feel a flash of almost apprehension but also great curiosity. I try to follow that. I wonder what will land on the page. In this state you're not exactly respon-sible. There's a sense that you're only *exploring*, that it's the object of your sketch leading you on, more than your own conscious decisions as an artist. It happens without you."

She has her bad art days, too, which is one reason she can extend genuine empathy to students. "It's more impor-tant to *do* than to *judge*," she says. "If I want to make and own a drawing but I don't feel like I know how that day, I'll do a contour or gesture or negative space drawing. I try to focus on one doable thing at a time. I say: I'm going to do just a contour drawing today. I'm going to *do* it well—not 'come up with a good product' but be fully engaged. And my drawing will capture some feeling of the place."

The spirit of place figures large in her creative vision. "I think that we become a little part of the places we visit, and they become a part of us," she says. "If you really are in some place experiencing it, you're going to encounter something original. To be creative, you just mess around and you keep your eyes open. Of course the work is original: you were *there*!"

As with her love of landscape, Jenny's fascination with the lives of organisms also animates her art. One year, in order to prepare herself to teach a new illustration class at UC Santa Cruz, she enrolled in a rigorous community col-lege course in zoology. Her lecture notes and lab journals rivaled meticulously illustrated textbooks in their precision and beauty. "There's no knowledge that feels as real or fas-cinating to me," she said to me one day in the middle of the semester. "It just seems like the stuff we're supposed to know."

At home, she keeps files of reference photographs and student drawings, as well as what she calls "small masterpieces"—exquisitely drawn cartoons, product wrappers, commercial illustrations. At holiday time, her family and close friends receive homemade gifts: memory game tiles featuring bits of her artwork, colorful jars of seventeen types of beans accompanied by hand-lettered soup recipes, hand-sewn miniature stuff sacks in a rainbow of colors. She has a binder full of clipped magazine photos, stored in plastic sleeves, with which she creates striking collage postcards to send to friends. She designs and sews her own sketchbook covers and zippered pouches for sketching equipment. Among the "toys" she carries into the field is a tiny handmade set of laminated cards bearing samples of her favorite calligraphic styles.

She frequently stays up all night preparing handouts and lesson plans. "Exposing the thing you love the most to the daily grind is like washing your lover's dirty socks," she says. "When you do it and teach it for a living, the feeling of making art is *going* to change. You have to let it. And ideally, it comes to a place you never would have come to if you'd kept the dailiness at bay. The real art is taking the thing you've chosen to immerse yourself in and learning to play within it. It's like constantly trying to charm, seduce, and win over someone who already knows you."

Years of Jenny's friendship and collegial inspiration have changed my relationship to my own work. My journal pages begin to seem incomplete with no drawing or graphic play. I'm finding my way to a sense of grace on the page—learning how to respect open space and how to let line dance with curve, thick with thin, dark with light.

Drawing becomes a metaphor for living—not in some abstract, cerebral way, but in my bones. The physicalness of sketching shifts my muscle memory—the breath, the flow of blood, the way my eye apprehends the world and the way my mind and heart interpret it. As I draw, I begin to think in the language of visual relationships. I enter into a state of trancelike focus, peaceful and buzzing. The words that fall on my page alongside the drawings are more fluid and honest; they capture my observations more accurately; they touch on truths I need to know.

One day Jenny put a line by Georgia O'Keeffe on the blackboard in her classroom: "When you take a flower in your hand and really look at it, it's your world for the moment. I want to give that world to someone else." An anthem for those of us who write, draw, and teach.

CB
sunday system
sadie in bed
1/30/13

Interstate Grace

Freeways make lousy vantage points for the arid West. They bypass the best landscapes, trash the ones they traverse, and bring out the worst in one's fellow travelers. Or so I was thinking as I baked under the Nevada sun at an I-80 rest stop called "Forty-Mile Desert."

I'd made a pit stop on a late-summer solo drive across the Great Basin. Nineteenth-century pioneers died in this desert, said the interpretive sign, from exposure and thirst. A scattering of road-weary folks picnicked at concrete tables or stood squinting into the glare. They had the inward-turned look of idled interstate drivers, screening their private journeys on mental windshields.

The rest area's drinking fountain wasn't working, but I had a full water bottle back in my dusty Toyota. I reached into my jeans pocket for the keys . . . nothing there. I tried the other pockets. Then, as I approached the car, I spotted my keys through the side window—sitting on the driver's seat.

All of the little station wagon's five doors were locked; all of the windows were shut tight. My shade hat and wallet were in the car. So were my journal, road food, and books. I considered asking another traveler for help—then reconsidered. A break-in expert, if I could find one, might prove an unreliable rescuer.

I used the pay phone to punch in a free operator call. Asking for the nearest auto club road service office, I remembered the membership card in my imprisoned wallet. While I braced for an argument with an officious clerk, the dispatcher from Reno came on. I explained my predicament.

She gave her name: Tracy. "Oh, what a bummer!" she said. "That won't do." The closest town was Lovelock, she said, and she could have a truck to me in half an hour. "Look, are you uncomfortable in the meantime? Does it seem like a hairy situation?" I said the rest stop seemed safe enough in daylight. Tracy urged me to call her back if I saw any threatening-looking characters and she would summon the highway patrol.

I perched on the car's hood and waited, watching scruffy blackbirds peck at crumbs. Carcinogenic sunshine pounded down on a parking lot littered with dog shit and broken glass. Garbage cans overflowed with discarded diapers and fast-food wrappers.

From a concrete picnic table laden with a gigantic cooler and bags of potato chips, a gaunt, sallow-looking couple with several scrawny children gazed my way. Their hard stares seemed to convey missionary disapproval. I thought I must seem heathenish in their eyes: a solitary middle-aged woman with short-cropped hair, loitering at a rest stop, her dusty car plastered with bumper stickers from public radio stations and enviro groups. I hoped they weren't scheming to save my soul.

At another table, a pair of tough-looking guys in their twenties with tattoos, leather jackets, and five-day whiskers sucked down beers, their Harleys parked nearby. They glanced at me occasionally, talking and laughing with each other in voices too low to decode. I pretended not to notice.

Finally, a yellow-and-blue tow truck pulled into the rest stop, and I waved it over. Three teenagers in coveralls emerged. The boy in charge fished a break-in kit from the truck and started jimmying the lock on my driver's-side door. He grunted and cussed and sweated for twenty minutes. His partner tried the passenger side, to no avail.

I glanced over at the skinny family: the mother was staring intently at me now, speaking to her two small sons. The boys began walking toward me, each clutching a little rectangular object. Miniature Bibles, I surmised. When they drew closer, I saw that what they carried were juice boxes, the kind with the plastic straw attached by a dollop of glue. The taller boy, about ten years old, proffered his, asking, "Would you like this, to drink while you wait?"

When I thanked the boy, he insisted that I accept the drink his little brother carried as well—"for later, in case you need it." No mention of Our Lord. "Thanks a lot," I said again and peeked over at the parents, who looked on nervously. When I waved, their drawn faces broke into smiles.

Meanwhile, my would-be saviors were shaking their heads. I dreaded the words I knew were coming: "Sorry, lady, you'll have to break a window or tow it to a locksmith back in Reno."

Then one of the leather-clad bikers sauntered over. "Okay if I try?" he asked. By this time the Lovelock guys were glad for anybody's help. "Sure," shrugged the older one. Motorcycle Dude accepted a tool and went to work. He had the door open in seconds.

"Wow, thanks," I said to his retreating back. "No problem," he called over his shoulder. "I bet my buddy I could open your car for you in less than a minute."

The mechanics piled into their truck and headed back to Lovelock. The bikers climbed on their motorcycles and roared away. I slid behind the wheel and took a last look around the desolate rest stop. The air was cooling now. The lowering sun bathed the picnic area in an apricot glow, and a flock of blackbirds, softly chuckling, lifted into the sky.

LIVING TOGETHER

Getting Along

People, I just want to say, you know, can't we all just get along?
—Rodney Glen King, third day of L.A. riots in response to jury
acquittal of the police officers who beat him, May 1, 1992

It was after ten o'clock on a weekday night, and the Santa Cruz campus of the University of California was quiet. As I came out of the night class I had been teaching, I glimpsed light flooding from the windows of one of the college dining halls. Peering in, I saw a thick crowd, mostly students of color, their eyes fixed on two men speaking from the stage. A flyer plastered to the door announced an appearance by two former Black Panthers.

Just as I decided to enter, a young African American woman leaned back against the door from inside, cracking it open as if to let some air into the crowded hall. I began to slip past her into the room, but she barred my way with an outstretched arm, barking in a stage whisper: "Do you want to come in? You have to be searched."

"For what?" I asked.

"Security," she growled impatiently. "Are you coming in or not?" The woman's voice bristled with hostility; she glared at me with such disdain that my head swam. Perhaps she was exhausted after a long day; perhaps she had already dealt with too many hassles that evening. Perhaps I was projecting my own unconscious assumptions, reading more antagonism into her tone than was really there. In any case, two facts leapt to the forefront of my awareness: I was white; she was black—and, to me, our interaction suddenly seemed scripted by those facts.

Too tired to deal thoughtfully with this scenario, knowing the presentation would end soon anyway, I left. But the experience had a familiar feel. It kicked me back to a time thirty years earlier, when I was part of a social experiment that gave rise to countless unresolved encounters between me and black students and that forced me—then and ever since—to think about the question later posed by Rodney King: *Can we get along?*

Late in the fall of 1968, I stood outside the girls' bathroom on the asphalt playground of Columbus School in Berkeley. I was in the sixth grade, and I was crying. The teacher on yard duty, a tall, angular white woman wearing a tight-fitting ribbed orange turtleneck and a peace-sign pendant, leaned over me, her face pushing into mine. I could see the pocks and pores in the skin of her long face and the smear of her bright lipstick. She had short-cropped reddish hair and wore bangly, ostentatiously African earrings that swung back and forth as she talked. While peering down at me, she kept an eye on the two girls who had hassled me in the bathroom; they were flanking her, looking both defiant and scared.

"What exactly happened? What were you doing? Were you *peeing*?" the teacher demanded. Standing in her shadow on the concrete apron outside the girls' bathroom, I felt both embarrassed and ashamed. She seemed determined to quiz me in the most personally detailed way, as if she had just learned the importance of being up front with children about intimate matters. Why was she interrogating *me* and not the two other girls? I couldn't tell if she was trying to protect me or punish me.

It was recess. I had been alone in the dirty tiled bathroom that smelled of stale cigarette smoke and girl-sweat. As I sat in the middle stall, I heard the door swing open and two girls enter, talking and laughing. Big girls, from the sound of them. The swagger in their talk told me that they were tough kids from the flats. They noticed my feet under the stall door. "What's your name, girl?" one of them demanded. I spoke it shyly, hating the indelible soft prissiness in my own voice and knowing that these girls understood, just from the way I uttered those two syllables, that I was a white kid bused down to Columbus from the hills.

They decided to have some fun with me. Entering the two stalls flanking mine, they stood on the toilet rims, grabbed the tops of the metal stall dividers, and hoisted themselves up so they could peer down on me from either side. Looking up, I saw that one of them was Chicana and the other black; both were large and womanly for sixth-graders. Recognizing my compromised position, they laughed, called me names, and cracked nasty jokes. One tossed her glowing cigarette butt down at me; it grazed my hair as it fell to the floor. I heard the quiet sizzle as a few strands of my thin straight hair curled into brittle, acrid straw.

"*Stop* it," I protested through my tears, regretting the petulant whine in my tone, feeling impotent and ridiculous. "*Don't.* Leave me *alone.*" Finally, they eased up and left the bathroom; I finished, washed my hands, and followed shortly after. I didn't relish the idea of telling on the girls—a sure way to clinch my status in their eyes as a pampered sissy, a tattler, a member of the enemy camp. But when I spotted the yard-duty teacher nearby, I realized that I wanted vindication and some kind of adult protection.

I got the woman's attention and pointed out my two tormentors. They hadn't gone far—as if they were resigned to being caught and thought they might as well get it over with. The teacher peered at me in what looked like hostile distress, as if she wanted to pretend the whole thing hadn't happened. But after grilling me, she hauled all three of us off to the principal.

A black man with tired-looking eyes, he gave each of us a chance to talk. I wanted to play down the whole episode, but he made me tell the story from my point of view, while the other two listened. He also heard each of them out. They claimed they hadn't meant any harm, were only trying to have a little fun. He knew the girls by name: Charlene and Regina. Like a fond but disappointed father, he spoke to them in a stern, weary voice. He made them apologize to me, gave them a few hours of detention, and sent us all away. After that, I saw Charlene or Regina in the halls from time to time, and we exchanged nods of recognition. Neither girl expressed any detectable hostility toward me; sometimes they even called out a neutral hello.

I am still grateful to that principal. With compassion and equanimity, he managed to defuse the haze of blame and fear that our little group trailed into his office. I like to think that all three of us girls—and perhaps also the yard-duty teacher—learned something useful from his example. If more of Berkeley's school administrators and faculty had possessed such wisdom, the city's fledgling desegregation project might have made more headway.

And then again, maybe not.

During that year at Columbus School, there were flare-ups and fistfights daily on the playground and in the halls— often among students from the flats, sometimes between them and the mostly white hill kids. Most of the white teachers who had come to Columbus from the hill schools seemed to have no clue what to do about these confrontations. They had no training and little experience with angry, physically defiant children. They were not prepared for the hostility that would meet an invasion of mostly white, middle-class strangers into a school set among poor, working-class neighborhoods.

Many of these white adults had harbored rosy hopes of a grand racial unification—led by the innocent children, who would prove to the jaded older generation that the color of a person's skin makes no difference in human relationships. It must have been hard to have those hopes dashed. The teacher who grilled me on the playground that day seemed to resent me for bringing my problems to her attention, as if I had personally sullied her vision of racial integration. Or perhaps she just felt fearful and bewildered. She was not the only one. When fights erupted in the hallways, the other white teachers would pretend not to notice—turning their backs or quickly shutting their classroom doors. They acted as clueless as I felt.

In retrospect, it seems to me as if nobody ever fully thought through the implications of the desegregation plan that brought busloads of white fourth-through-sixth-graders to Columbus that year—a plan that was implemented at every one of Berkeley's elementary schools. Until 1968, de facto segregation characterized most of those schools. If your family lived in the quiet, verdant Berkeley Hills, you attended school with your middle- and upper-middle-class neighbors—most of them white, a few Asian American, a tiny minority from other ethnic groups. If you lived in the flats, the other-side-of-the-tracks neighborhoods close to the city's industrial bay shore, you attended a flats school, dominated by litter-strewn asphalt and cyclone fences and populated by mostly black- and brown-skinned people.

There were some exceptions. A handful of schools in the residential zones where the hills and the flats met were host to a rainbow mix of children—kids whose families already shared the same neighborhoods. For more contrived reasons, the nearly all-white student populations in the hill schools included a darker face or two from time to time. When I was attending the second grade at Oxford Elementary, there was one black kid in the entire school: a shy, quiet boy I'll call Stanley. He seemed sweet and smart, but he rarely talked much, in or out of class, and he often appeared to be on the verge of tears. I had heard that Stanley actually lived in the flats but that his mother worked days in the hills. She may have cleaned houses, or perhaps she was a visiting nurse. I saw her once in a while when she came to pick Stanley up—a large, dignified woman in a crisp white uniform. She had apparently arranged with the school district to take Stanley to Oxford School on her way to work every day—so that he could be closer to her and perhaps so that he could receive the same education as the white kids were getting.

One day in class, our ancient, severe second-grade teacher, Mrs. Taylor, taught us a rhyme: "Eenie, meenie, miney, moe . . . ." In the version I already knew from playing schoolyard games, the next line was "Catch a tiger by the toe." But Mrs. Taylor substituted a word I'd never heard before: "nigger." I thought this must be some other kind of animal, like a tiger but different. At home that evening, I innocently sang Mrs. Taylor's version for my mother and father. When I came to the new part, they looked horrified. They hastily explained to me what "nigger" meant, how it was used, and that it was a word I should never, ever say. Stricken, I thought about Stanley. What had gone through his mind as Mrs. Taylor blithely taught us to say "nigger"? What, if anything, had gone through hers?

When I entered the fourth grade, my family moved to a larger house a few blocks from the old one, crossing a school district boundary. Cragmont Elementary was perched on a steep hillside along steeply pitched Marin Avenue, a tree-lined boulevard that sweeps several miles straight up from the bayside flats to the crest of the Berkeley Hills. Some two dozen black kids were bused to Cragmont from the flats each morning and returned home after school each afternoon. I never learned the origins of this pilot busing program or how the kids were selected for it. They were farmed out into different classrooms, but at lunch and recess they came together, talking and joking among themselves.

One of those kids, Trudelle, was in my fourth-grade class. Like Stanley in the second grade, she was quiet, shy and polite in class, almost as if she were trying hard not to be noticed—as if, I imagined, her parents had told her that she must be on her best behavior. At recess, though, she laughed and cut up with her friends from the flats. I liked Trudelle. She had a creamy voice and mocha-colored skin, a kind, dimply smile and a twinkle in her eyes. I wondered if she resented us white kids, who lived within walking distance of the school and therefore owned it in a way she and her friends could not. Trudelle and I were the shortest kids in our fourth-grade class, which gave us a kind of bond. We exchanged a few words from time to time, but something—the mutual mystery of our home lives, the untold differences between us—kept us wary, as if we stood on either side of a moat a hundred yards wide.

My fifth-grade teacher at Cragmont, Mrs. Schaeffer, emanated genuine excitement about the Berkeley Unified School District's plan to integrate all of the kindergarten-through-sixth-grade schools the following year. A fervently progressive white Southerner from Tennessee, she pinned up photographs of civil-rights activists around the classroom and taught us about the history of slavery and the struggle for racial equality in America. We learned about slave ships and slave markets, Harriet Tubman, Dred Scott, Marcus Garvey, Nat Turner, Thurgood Marshall, Rosa Parks, the Freedom Riders, *Brown v. Board of Education*, the 1963 civil rights march on Washington, Martin Luther King Jr., Malcolm X. Mrs. Schaeffer sang us blues and folk songs in her Tennessee lilt, accompanying herself on her twelve-string guitar, and she played us a recording of Dr. King's "I Have a Dream" speech. We believed, along with Mrs. Schaeffer and most of our parents, that the integration plan would be a way to bring the people of our town together.

That March, the school handed out buttons to pin on our clothes: TOGETHERNESS, they proclaimed; EQUALITY, INTEGRATION—in psychedelic chartreuse block letters on an electric-blue field. We wore them with pride. One grade at a time, the district sent us across San Francisco Bay for overnight retreats at a youth camp, Camp Bothin ("bo-THEEN"), in the hills of Marin County, where we would meet some of our future classmates from the other side of the tracks.

It was a sunny, breezy day when we arrived, and the spring-green coastal hills were studded with wildflowers. That night, my friends from Mrs. Schaeffer's class and I shared sleeping quarters with our future schoolmates on cots arranged side by side along a terra cotta floor, the mullioned glass doors open to the fragrant night air. The two counselors in charge of my dorm were black teenagers, probably students from Berkeley High School. Smokey was light-skinned and playful, Mary dark and serious. They listened to Motown music on transistor radios. To me they seemed impossibly grown up, beautiful and intense.

On the afternoon of the retreat's second day, we milled around in the sunshine on the camp's unpaved parking lot, loading gear into school buses, preparing for the forty-minute ride back to Berkeley. Then somebody made an announcement, and the crowd grew still: Dr. King had been shot dead.

A teacher asked for five minutes of silence—normally out of the question in a crowd of eleven-year-olds. There was some tentative shuffling on the gravel, students migrating quietly from their assigned places to stand with friends. Adults wore grave, stricken expressions; some looked angry. We students—several dozen black, brown, yellow, and white schoolchildren—stood mute and uncertain, each trying to make some kind of private sense of the news, avoiding each other's gaze in the early April sunshine.

My own silence was troubled by numb confusion. I knew that we might not have been here in the first place, embarking on this righteous experiment, were it not for Dr. King. But I didn't know how to reach out to my black counterparts who glanced sideways at me with mistrust and suspicion. I knew they had no idea how to reach out to me and maybe no desire to do so. Not even Smokey or Mary, for all their tough sweetness and wisdom, could show us the way.

When I think back on it four decades later, having learned more about Dr. King and the complex political reality he challenged, I am struck again by his tremendous audacity. A black man only three generations removed from slavery, he understood better than most white Berkeley educators the heartache that we were in for, a city trying to heal an ailing community through school desegregation. But he put his faith in the possibility that we and other communities around the nation could eventually succeed.

"When our days become dreary with low-hovering clouds and our nights become darker than a thousand midnights,"

King the orator had sung out, "we will know that we are living in the creative turmoil of a genuine civilization struggling to be born." Because of him, and the battalions of civil-rights activists who gave life to the dream he proclaimed so eloquently, that same faith beat in my eleven-year-old heart. Whatever else I felt that day at Camp Bothin, I knew beyond doubt—even if I could not have put it into words—that what we in Berkeley were trying to do was essentially necessary and right.

That first year of integration didn't take Berkeley's schoolchildren, let alone the community as a whole, much beyond pain and puzzlement. The buses rolled, but logistics seemed the only aspect of the plan that worked. After a troubled year at Columbus, I went on to Martin Luther King Jr. Junior High School, one of two junior highs in town, both long integrated de facto. At King, black animosity toward white kids sharpened its teeth. The aggressive outbreaks were more violent and the anger more desperate, complicated by an edge of adolescent sexuality and a nascent drug scene. One day as I walked down the urine-tinged concrete stairwell in a between-classes press of bodies, a black boy I didn't know grabbed my breast hard through my sweatshirt and twisted it painfully, muttering "*White bitch.*" Another time during the shuffle between classes, a black kid kicked the heel of my wooden-soled clog from behind, sending a shock up my leg and launching the shoe toward the hallway's high ceiling. There were more cigarettes in my hair, more hateful epithets.

By the time I arrived at Berkeley High, the city's large single public high school, the heat of racial aggression had cooled—but thanks only to a tacit agreement that racial and socioeconomic groups would pretty much keep to themselves. I have no idea how this came about, only that an uneasy peace descended with the voluntary separation. Berkeley High School in the 1970s was integrated in name only.

When my politically progressive mother and father talk about Berkeley's 1968 elementary school desegregation, they recall it bitterly. As an emblem of the entire year, they remember more than anything else "the time those tough girls brutalized you in the bathroom." Of course my parents were frightened for their children. They resented the difficulties that my siblings and I were forced to face, and they worried that our schooling was being compromised. They returned home enraged from school board meetings, where their well-meaning liberal white neighbors refused to entertain discussions about black violence against white students, as if such incidents could be nothing but dangerous racist lies.

I empathize with my parents, but in spite of everything, I do not regret my experiences at Columbus School. They opened my eyes to a world of social discord that affects every person in this country—even those privileged enough to avoid its most directly damaging impact. I do think, though, that unless we look more closely at the lessons of those difficult and exasperating times, they will not have moved us forward in our quest to get along.

Denying racial animosity will not make it go away. We can close the classroom door, but the fistfight in the hallway will go on. We have to stop expecting children to do a job that only an entire community or society can accomplish. And we ignore at our peril the power of social class as a player in the tensions between races. Charlene and Regina's beef with me was not just about the color of my skin. They were pissed off in part because they understood that, physically small and weak though I might be, my social position as the child of Berkeley Hills professionals conferred a relatively formidable privilege that they, a couple of working-class kids from the flats, could never experience.

I don't have answers. I began this essay years ago and have been pulling it out of the drawer periodically ever since—trying to figure out what I need to learn from pondering that chapter of my childhood. Occasionally, a new encounter offers another smidgeon of insight.

On an evening some years ago, I emerged from the Nickelodeon Theater in Santa Cruz, California, after a showing of the documentary film *Hoop Dreams*. The movie follows two inner-city African American teenagers, talented basketball players, as they try to make their way out of dead-end lives into an NBA future. Anyone watching this documentary is invited into intimate contact with the athletes and with their families, coaches, and friends. It is impossible to see *Hoop Dreams*, I think, without absorbing the black teens' fears and ambitions. Even though I have never played basketball, I walked out of the theater into the waning light of a clear evening filled with empathy toward those two remarkable young men and admiration for their struggles. I felt connected to them as if they were my brothers.

On my way to the parking lot, I saw, half a short block away, a young black man walking toward me. In response to this sight—uncommon in Santa Cruz—my instant, unmediated reaction was one of recognition and love. This man was a stranger to me, but the emotions that still flooded me from seeing *Hoop Dreams* were spilling out into the world to color our brief encounter.

Immediately, I realized the rarity of this moment. The sight of a black man coming my way on a city street usually, to be honest, conjures up inchoate anxiety. At best, goes the subconscious logic, he must resent or mistrust me because I'm white; at worst, I imagine, he's poor and criminally inclined and a threat to my safety. For once free of such prejudices, with my heart opened wide, I could clearly see the deep-seated racism that I normally carry everywhere.

I have long given lip service to the "politically correct" notion that, like anybody raised in the United States, I am bound to possess internalized racist attitudes. But the impact of *Hoop Dreams* was to momentarily replace this intellectual awareness with visceral understanding. My brief racial gestalt shift reminded me of an epiphany that actor and comedian Richard Pryor reported experiencing the first time he got off a plane in a postcolonial African country. Surrounded by that nation's black-skinned citizens, Pryor thought to himself, Oh my god: there are *no niggers* here.

Pryor's revelation dawned when he found himself among members of his own race, free of a dominant white population, in a country not built on black slavery. Mine arose when I was momentarily relieved of my own racial stereotypes. What the two experiences have in common is a transcendent if fleeting vision of life unencumbered by racism. On that evening outside the movie theater, I experienced, ever so briefly, what it might be like to live in a world where empathy and respect supplant suspicion and fear.

There's a lesson here for those who seek to transform a racist society: we need the arts. Film, dance, drama, song, sculpture, paintings, poetry, and fiction have the power to get inside us, to change the way we experience the world—and thus the way we act. *Hoop Dreams* worked on my worldview as the writings of James Baldwin, Toni Morrison, Alice Walker, Audre Lorde and others have done over the years, effecting incremental yet profoundly important shifts in my understanding.

Art makes a difference, and so, as the world was reminded in November of 2008, can politics. The days following the

U.S. presidential election felt to me like my *Hoop Dreams* moment writ large. On city streets, I gazed at black and mixed-race fellow citizens and suddenly saw people who looked less like me than like my president-elect. In their eyes, I thought I detected pride, dignity, and a sense of enfranchisement that had not been there before. And the universe seemed to tilt in a new direction.

Berkeley in the late 1960s taught me this: it doesn't help to pretend that race-related problems are as simple as black and white—or Day-Glo blue and green. Integration and togetherness are not slogans to be plastered on lapel pins for children to wear to school. If we are serious about those goals, then we have to create safe places where each of us, all ages and colors, cultures and classes, can tell our own stories and listen to others' truths—ugly and messy as they may feel, complex and troublesome as they may indeed be. If this process goes no further than the principal's office, then we will never learn to get along.

Staircase to Nowhere

My education was interrupted only by my schooling.

—Winston Churchill

One afternoon several years ago, while driving across town on a series of frustrating errands, I came to a stop behind a long line of cars waiting for a train to cross the road. The candy-striped gates were down—lights flashing, bells clanging. But no train came. Five minutes passed; more cars lined up behind me. Another few minutes, and still no train. Stuck in place with nowhere to go, I let my mind wander to the events that had brought me to this juncture.

It began when a local high school teacher I knew—I'll call her Diane—approached me about a guest instructor gig. Diane had recently revived her public school's Gifted and Talented Education program—GATE for short. GATE's goal is to provide learning opportunities for capable students who aren't sufficiently challenged by the regular curriculum. Diane even managed what you might think would be the hardest part: she got money so she could hire local professionals to teach in the program. She had school funds set aside for a series of weekend class offerings on a variety of subjects, and she set about finding qualified professionals from the community to teach them. Knowing of my background as a science journalist, she invited me to lead a GATE class on writing about science. I had taught high school before moving on to college-level instruction, and I welcomed the opportunity to work with that age group again.

It looked easy at first. Diane asked me to submit a course proposal. I designed a series of four Saturday afternoon science writing workshops and sent her a detailed description. "Great," said Diane. "I'd love to take that class myself. I'm sure some students will be interested."

So I started planning my workshops in earnest. Meanwhile, as Diane directed, I submitted a pay request, outlining the number of hours I expected to work, what I intended to do with the time, how much I wanted to be paid per hour, and how I was qualified for the post. Next, I was sent two forms to fill out—one in quintuplicate—specifying all of this in even greater detail. In passing, I noticed that one of the forms had a question for Diane. The district wanted to know what steps she was taking to avoid hiring any more outside experts in the future. As it turns out, the district need not have worried . . . but I'm getting ahead of myself. I completed and submitted all of the forms.

Assuming, along with Diane, that I had now been hired, I taught my first two workshops. The students were great: cheerful and talkative and bright, and motivated enough to give up their Saturday afternoons to improve their writing. But then came an apologetic phone call from Diane: "I'm so sorry," she said. "I just learned that in order to get paid to work with kids, you have to be fingerprinted. It's a precaution, to make sure you aren't a convicted child molester or something. You just have to drop in at the district office and they'll take care of it."

Fair enough, I thought. So I drove across town to the shiny new district administration building. I found the employee Diane had told me to see. But this person, it turned out, couldn't actually take my fingerprints. She could only do the paperwork required to *set me up* for fingerprinting. She asked for my social security number, examined my driver's license, asked me some questions, and typed up a couple of forms—one of them in triplicate. I was to take these forms and submit them to the county education office ten miles away in an adjacent city, where I would then, the employee said, be fingerprinted.

At this other office, she continued, I should retrieve the middle copy of the completed triplicate form, and then I was to bring it back to her at the district office. Once the federal government had confirmed my non-child-molester status, she would help me fill out a green time sheet indicating the hours I worked. I realized that I would be expected to lie on this sheet, since I had already put in some teaching time. Legally, I wasn't supposed to have started until after my fingerprints had been cleared.

There was one additional catch. Before filling out the time sheet, I would have to produce my Social Security card. Not just the number—the physical card. I have not seen that little piece of paper since I was a high school student myself. It's probably long since rotted in some landfill. Moreover, nobody—not the Internal Revenue Service, not the U.S. State Department when it issued my passport, not the loan officer at the bank or the headmaster who hired me to teach in a private high school—has ever needed to see it. But the school district could not put me on its payroll until I showed my card. Before I took my fingerprint form back to the district office to fill out the green timesheet, I would have to go to the downtown Social Security office and fill out the application for a replacement card.

This is where things stood as I sat idling at the railroad junction. I turned off the ignition, sighing over this obstacle course of a day. My thoughts drifted to stories Diane had told me: one anecdote after another about ill-fated attempts by teachers in the district to enrich their students' education. There was the purchase order for student tickets to a poetry reading, drawn on ample GATE funds, that didn't materialize until six weeks from the time it had been requested—long after the reading had taken place. There was the famous writer who withdrew her agreement to meet with students when she learned she'd have to be fingerprinted. And so on. I was reminded of *Up the Down Staircase*, Bel Kaufman's funny-sad best-selling novel—published in 1964 and later made into a hit movie—about a spirited public school teacher slamming into endless administrative roadblocks.

Finally, I gave up on the railroad gates, realizing they must be out of order. I started my car, pulled a U-turn over the highway divider, and doubled back to bypass the blocked crossing. I kept teaching the science writing class. Eventually, after I had driven more miles around the county skirting roadblocks, the district paid me for my services. Meanwhile, Diane had spent so many frustrating hours running interference for me and for this program that she vowed never to try to hire another outside instructor. At the end of the school year, she quit coordinating the GATE program.

If I were more paranoid, I might assume that this was the result the school administration had explicitly hoped for all along. They did, after all, ask Diane that pointed question, on the quintuplicate personnel form, about how she planned to avoid adding to the district payroll in the future. Now she was conveniently burning out and giving up on the whole project.

More likely, this is just another sad story about a bureaucracy doing what's necessary to comply with audits and regulations—and, in the process, thwarting the enterprise it is set up to support. There's got to be a better way to build a staircase.

Between the Closet and the Flames

As a college student in 1979, I wore my "Radcliffe Lesbians" T-shirt to what was then called the San Francisco Gay Freedom Day Parade. On the shirt's insignia, two women danced, hands clasped and hair flying. The Latin motto read *Ex cubiculo, in sartagem*: "Out of the closet, into the frying pan."

A woman about twenty-five years my senior spotted the shirt and squeezed toward me through the crowd. She grasped my shoulders, surveyed the dancing lovers emblazoned on my chest, and gave me a wry look. "When I was at Radcliffe," she said, "there was no such thing as the Radcliffe Lesbians." There were tears on her face.

It was true: the climate had changed. By 1979, lesbians and gay men on college campuses around the country were beginning to affirm their sexual orientation in public. They were finding solidarity and pride, thanks to pioneering activists who had chosen the frying pan over the closet. I understood the envy of that anonymous older woman disappearing into the crowd. Compared with her generation's closeted past, young, educated lesbians in 1979 had plenty to be grateful for.

But the struggle for gay rights was still far from won—and, in any case, the T-shirt I wore to the parade didn't tell my whole story. I wasn't, strictly speaking, a lesbian. I was attracted sexually and emotionally to both women and men.

I was and am bisexual. As I celebrated camaraderie with my gay and lesbian brothers and sisters on that Gay Freedom Day more than three decades ago, I felt paradoxically invisible.

Bisexual women sought out Radcliffe Lesbians meetings in the late 1970s because we were alienated by the university's misogynist, homophobic culture—an atmosphere so unsafe that in mixed company, group members avoided speaking our organization's name aloud, substituting the moniker "Sunshine Girls." We sought sisterhood in this small lesbian community of no more than a couple dozen women—part social club, part political organization. But if a bisexual dared acknowledge her true orientation to other members of the group, she was likely to encounter not warmth and acceptance but suspicion and hostility.

We were not "real lesbians"; we were seen as potential traitors. As lovers we were considered risky, for we might turn to men, abandoning our lesbian identities as well as particular relationships. If we were bold enough to wear the organization's T-shirt in public, some of our lesbian sisters saw us as playacting. As bisexuals we presumably had the option of falling back on heterosexual privilege: we could show off our liaisons with men in order to preserve our mainstream respectability.

That privilege is real, but so is the need to be recognized and understood for all that we are. In the words of bisexual activist Lani Kaahumanu, "Coming out as a bisexual is not . . . done to acquire or flaunt heterosexual privilege. I am bisexual because I am drawn to particular people regardless of gender. It doesn't make me wishy-washy, confused, untrustworthy, or more sexually liberated. It makes me bisexual."

It's a diverse group. While by definition bisexuals are attracted to people of both sexes, not all of us act in both directions. We may enter into straight marriages or committed same-sex relationships. We may be monogamous, promiscuous, or celibate. For us, gender alone doesn't determine whether or not a relationship has sexual possibility, but this doesn't mean that we lead frenzied orgiastic lives. On the contrary, we may approach love, passion, romance, intimacy, family, and friendship in especially conscious, thoughtful ways. Our proclivities not only "double our chances for a Saturday night date," as Woody Allen put it; they force us to make considered decisions about our sexual involvements and the social pressures that influence them.

We have come a long way since 1979. Contemporary "queer" politics transcend the narrower outlook of nascent liberation movements. "Gay" organizations have given way to "GLBTQ"—"gay, lesbian, bisexual, transgendered, queer" or, sometimes, "questioning." Thanks to the brave efforts of intersex scholars and activists, there is even a dawning awareness that anatomical gender itself doesn't always fall neatly into two distinct categories. Healthy sexuality takes many forms, and as that diversity becomes increasingly apparent, the "you're either with us or against us" attitude toward bisexuals has eased up.

I still have my Radcliffe Lesbians shirt. The black cotton has faded to charcoal; countless washings have thinned it to translucency. It's the softest, most comfortable T-shirt I own, though unfortunately it no longer accommodates my expanding body. Even when I could still fit into the shirt, the decision to wear it around town was never straightforward, and I often left it in the drawer. Instead of putting it on, I'd fasten an enameled copper pin to my lapel: a blue-and-lavender triangle superimposed over a pink one. Few people recognize this symbol of bisexuality—but if you see me wearing it, I hope you'll ask what it means.

Cultural Cosmetics / Cosmetic Culture

When I was about ten years old, a young adult friend of my parents went to a cosmetic surgeon for a "nose job." Her original nose featured a raised contour across the bridge; the one she emerged with, after the bandages and bruises had disappeared and the swelling had gone down, sloped in a dainty curve toward its upturned tip. Though the friend appeared to be delighted with her new nose, I felt uncomfortable gazing at it. I couldn't help imagining what the surgeon had had to do to effect such a transformation. Besides, the newly sculpted organ looked too insubstantial to allow the friend to breathe properly; its concave profile seemed on the verge of sinking still further into her face, even disappearing altogether.

I recall my parents' attitude at the time as one of mild disapproval. If I remember right, they intimated that spending money and risking one's safety for such an operation was at best a vain and frivolous act. In the case of their friend—Jewish like us—it also represented a betrayal of ethnic heritage. Along with many other Mediterranean, Middle Eastern, and Eastern European people, some Jews have bumpy noses, a trait often singled out by bigots as a focus of ridicule, exclusion, and hatred. If the term had been current in the early 1960s, my parents might have said that the friend's nose job was an expression of internalized anti-Semitism. And they probably would have been at least partly right.

A few years later, I began to flirt with the idea of a cosmetic operation of my own. By age fifteen, I had developed pendulous, heavy breasts that caused me a great deal of physical discomfort and interfered with my attempts at athletic activity—even when I wore two industrial-strength bras. On my small frame, my expanding bust also made it hard to find attractive clothes that fit.

I had complicated feelings about my breasts. Beyond the soreness and chafing and posture problems, they caused me aesthetic grief. I had nothing against breasts in general: I loved the graceful curves of small, shapely ones, and I could appreciate generously proportioned ones on an ample woman's body. But try as I might to accept my own curves, I found them ungainly and ugly. I remember coming across a passage in a novel that portrayed a character's pillowy breasts as "blind and inflated, with nipples like a man's." The phrase described my own body so accurately that it burned itself indelibly into my memory.

At the same time, my chest frequently attracted catcalls from men on the street: cries less of admiration than of rapacity and aggression. On my way to a dance class on Bancroft Way in Berkeley one afternoon after school, negotiating thick crowds near the UC campus, I passed by a tall, scruffy man who made a show of scrutinizing my body and then declared to the world at large, "It may be little, but *it's got everything on it!*" My budding feminist consciousness registered this as a comically perfect example of the objectification of women. The tender girl in me wanted to cry.

Males I knew personally registered their own reactions, if behind my back. A friend told me that she'd overheard one of our high school classmates—someone I'd thought of as a mature, considerate guy—joking with his pals about my big "headlights." And then came the day when my two fellow driver training students missed class and I found myself on my own in a school-owned Ford Galaxie 500, seated at the wheel beside my middle-aged male driving instructor. He directed me to a lightly traveled road, and when I stopped there at a traffic light, he reached over from the passenger seat and cupped my right breast in his trembling hand. Then he withdrew from me almost immediately and pretended the incident hadn't happened.

In my revisionist fantasies a few decades after the fact, I tell the guy off in no uncertain terms, abandon him in the car, take a bus home, and report him to the school board. In reality, I was shocked and cowed into silence—because I felt deeply ashamed and ambivalent about my adolescent body and also because at the time I suffered from acute driving phobia. It was all I could do simply to operate a vehicle in traffic, gripped as I was by overwhelming anxiety, without having to chew out my instructor for perpetrating sexual abuse. I'm not even sure that concept had reached my consciousness back in 1974.

I consulted with a surgeon, who said I'd be a good candidate for breast reduction. My parents were understanding and supportive, without urging me either toward or away from the operation. But I ended up concluding that my motivations at the time were too conflicted. The hatred I felt toward my breasts as a teenager was a mix of my own physical misery and aesthetic sensibility on the one hand and my rage and pain at being targeted by a misogynist culture on the other. I was damned if I was going to lie on an operating table and have my body sliced open as a reaction to some idiotic men's behavior or in order to comply with profit-driven beauty standards. I vowed that if I were ever to choose surgery, it would be out of self-determination, as pure and powerful as I could muster.

That day did eventually come. In my early thirties, after exhaustive research and a successful campaign to persuade my insurance company to cover the cost, I underwent a "bilateral reduction mammoplasty." My mother and my boyfriend at the time accompanied me to the hospital. The surgeon was experienced and capable; he honored my request that he remove as much tissue as possible without jeopardizing the sensation or circulation in my breasts. The procedure went smoothly and the recovery was surprisingly easy; I never even took an aspirin.

People who have met me since that time would probably be surprised to learn that I had a breast reduction. My bust is bigger than I'd like it to be—but, even so, a good deal smaller than if I'd foregone the surgery. After carefully working through that decision over many years, I never regretted it.

The deliberation that I brought to this experience is nowhere to be seen in mainstream representations of cosmetic surgery. Collect a stack of today's supermarket newsstand magazines and extract all of the latest cosmetic surgery headlines and you'll find a litany not too different from the ones of the previous decade or the one before that: "New nose, new chin, new me!"; "A doctor drained my fat away"; "Breasts: bigger is better"; "At last I feel good about myself"; and, modestly, "A whole life makeover." The way they report this stuff, you'd think it entails no cultural or political dimension, no complexity whatsoever.

When, in my midtwenties, I entered a graduate program in science journalism, I found myself forced to decide whether to add my voice to that chorus. As luck would have it, my first invitation to write a feature-length magazine story came from a glossy regional rag that normally covered golf tournaments and restaurant openings. The editor, having noted a rash of recent national news stories about new developments in cosmetic surgery, wanted to run a story about how local doctors were reacting to the latest techniques.

I had yet to undergo my own operation at the time, but I had done plenty of thinking about medical interventions in appearance as a cultural issue, and the last thing I wanted to put out into the world was another plastic-surgery puff piece. Still, I couldn't resist the opportunity to publish my first full-length freelance magazine article. I took the assignment and interviewed a bunch of local cosmetic surgeons. Fortunately, I discovered a medically conservative streak in each of the doctors I spoke with and so found an editorial slant for the article that I could live with. I emphasized the irony inherent in a group of professionals dedicated, by definition, to making change (*plastic* derives from a Greek root meaning "to mold or influence"), who nevertheless urged caution and wariness upon their prospective patients. I let the surgeons convey this perspective through their own quotes, and I was thrilled to see my first feature in print.

But I wasn't through with the subject. Why, I continued musing, do so many people, especially women, feel compelled to pay large sums of money to have themselves cut and stitched into closer approximations of the currently acceptable "look"? And how, if we so desire, can we battle that compulsion in ourselves?

As I learned in the process of researching and reporting my article, unwanted features do not slip readily away like interchangeable Barbie-doll accessories; the process of wresting them from the body requires both skill and force. Nose jobs entail removing cartilage and bone—essentially, breaking the nose and pressing it back together again. Dermabrasion, a common way of removing facial marks, does to the skin what a sander does to a floor. Botox injections reduce facial wrinkling by paralyzing small muscles around the eyes and mouth—at the cost of one's full ability to register emotion on the face, and also, recent psychological research suggests, one's capacity to read emotional situations. Liposuction, or "fat vacuuming," sucks out localized fat deposits—such as the pronounced thighs, bellies and hips characteristic of many human females—and for the next couple of weeks leaves the patient feeling as if she's been kicked by a mule.

The brutality of these surgical offerings calls to mind a colorful mural I once admired in the anthropology wing of the National Museum of Natural History in Washington, D.C. A testimonial to the apparently universal human penchant for mutilation in the name of good looks, the painting depicts Filipino natives with teeth filed to shark points, New Guinea warriors with wasp waists elongated by constricting bands, and Amazonians with stretched lips and ear lobes. As I lingered before the mural, I heard museum visitors around me expressing appreciative disgust: "Hey, Joan, look at this!" They shook their heads and marveled at the oddities of human culture. "Why do these tribal people let themselves be mangled and maimed? And how on earth can they think it's attractive?" Like other viewers, I almost failed to notice the small, white-skinned figure tucked unobtrusively into a corner of the mural: a Caucasian male, clothed in mid-twentieth-century business garb, before and after a nose job.

I often wonder what I would do if I had been born into one of those native cultures but didn't want to file my teeth or cinch my waist. In a sense, we are all stuck with an exotic tribe. While to some extent our identity inexorably arises from our membership in a particular society, one of the challenges of living within it is to know how to buck its customs when they cut—literally—into our sense of self.

I am not suggesting that anyone with a carefully considered desire for cosmetic surgery should be deprived of the opportunity, as long as she understands its limitations and risks. In some cases, surgery can free a person of a crippling preoccupation with appearance. In my own case, it allowed for daily pleasure in inhabiting my body. I would never argue that cosmetic procedures should not be an option.

But under our current medical system, insurance rarely pays for hospital procedures deemed purely cosmetic, so it's only the wealthy who can truly "elect" to have these procedures. Moreover, we might want to ask ourselves about the messages that drive so many women (and, increasingly, men) to desperation about the way they look. Where do those messages come from, and do we need to listen?

"You are not alone," soothes one electrolysist's advertisement: studies show, it says, that over 80 percent of women have unwanted facial hair. If the great majority of women have it, one wonders, how has it become "unwanted"? What brilliant marketing strategy has turned a widespread trait into a perceived aberration? Why should anyone with hair anywhere, no matter how unusual, feel compelled to hide, remove, or bleach it?

We grow up with a horror of being physically different, whether that means deviating from a biological norm or from some racially and commercially determined standard. "Visions of beauty change in time, but basic body shapes do not," warns the advertisement of a California surgeon promoting fat vacuuming. If the trend toward slimness has left your basic shape behind, the ad implies, then you owe it to yourself and the people who must look at you to have the offending parts sucked away—enriching the surgeon in the process. In an appearance-conscious culture with restrictive criteria for attractiveness, physical features function almost like identity papers: without the coveted kind in our possession, it's sometimes difficult to convince strangers and even ourselves of our personal worth.

When going under the knife means capitulating to media-amplified voices that say we are unacceptable, perhaps it is time to look for another solution. One option is to perform a more political sort of surgery: to excise the censuring internalized voices and the scars they have left on our psyches. This is easier said than done. Stoically reminding oneself that "it's what's inside that counts" doesn't do the trick. The only medicine I have found so far to counteract my own aesthetic tunnel vision is the example set by others who carry their own birthmarks, double chins, and wrinkles with pride. I've taken particular inspiration from a few memorable college students who have taken my classes over the years. Extravagantly plump and fleshy, with bodies that wouldn't register on the mainstream beauty scale, these young women wear low-cut, tight-fitting clothes and showy jewelry. They smile broadly, speak with authority, and take up space with a sense of entitlement I never could have mustered at their age. They act as if they're beautiful and sexy—and they are.

There is no more powerful antidote for physical self-dislike than knowing someone who lives comfortably, even joyfully, inside her own body, beauty standards be damned. If we are looking for something to snatch us back from the cosmetic surgeon's doorstep, perhaps it's the lifetime support and example of friends, acquaintances, and other members of our communities who consciously celebrate the human form in all its outrageous diversity.

Love and Dread on the Lifeboat

The world is too dangerous for anything but truth and too small for anything but love.

—William Sloane Coffin

1. Trouble in Paradise

"I am really going to *miss* orange juice," lamented Elaine*, topping off her glass from a store-bought carton.

It was late June 2007. Four of us sat around a breakfast table set with plates of scrambled eggs, freshly baked bread with marmalade, strawberries just off the vine, handmade goat cheese. A border collie snoozed at our feet. Outside the French doors, summer rain fell through pearly skies onto a meticulously tended garden and chicken coop; beyond rose a forest of native maple and spruce. Thrush song and a wren's chatter laced the air.

"We do have the potted dwarf citrus in the Jacuzzi greenhouse," Elaine's husband reminded her. "Several varieties, two of each. They won't give as much juice as we're used to, but we won't be completely without."

My husband and I were visiting from California. Chuck had met Jim about twenty years before and admired the lively engineer's intellectual intensity. Jim eventually got to know Elaine, a school administrator, and they married; the four of us got together a few times. But before the friendship had a

---
* Names have been changed.

chance to gel, Jim and Elaine quit their jobs and moved away. For a few years, they had been cultivating a self-sufficient life in the Pacific Northwest. So when a summer teaching gig brought Chuck and me within a hundred miles, they invited us to see their uncommon home.

We were curious to witness the life we had been reading about. Since their move, contact between our households had consisted of email commentaries. Two or three times a week, Jim and Elaine forwarded columns and editorials that excoriated mainstream apathy, chronicled staggering losses, or warned of looming danger. As I scrolled down the daily email queue, their apocalyptic subject lines always snagged my attention: "30 Days to Absolute Tyranny!" "Black Friday: Why This One Is Especially Dark"; "Mother Nature Down for the Count"; "A Wake-up Call: Another 911." Other headers disparaged the misguided optimism of unwary citizens: "Must Read: 'Beyond Hope'"; "The Grim View from the Deck of the Titanic."

In appended messages, Elaine and Jim made their own opinions clear, predicting that post–Peak Oil dark times would be upon the United States far sooner than most of us wanted to believe. Before long, our lives would be severely disrupted by economic collapse, shortages of goods and energy, increasing ecological upheaval, and social mayhem. They predicted, too, that the last faint gasps of American democracy would soon be silenced in the tightening grip of a corporate-controlled police state.

In these missives and on their web site, Jim and Elaine likened their homestead to a lifeboat poised to leave a sinking *Titanic*. Working to furnish as much of their own water, power, and food as they possibly could, they were readying themselves for imminent cataclysm and urging others to do the same. Through their local community-sponsored radio station, they hosted a monthly interview program on self-sufficiency. Jim trained and served with the local volunteer fire department, while Elaine worked with a community emergency preparedness network. They regularly opened their home to visiting interns, providing protégés with room and board, library resources, and a curriculum on sustainable living.

To get to Jim and Elaine's, you turn off a rural road at a gate marked with a lifeboat insignia. The parking area tops a long, steep driveway, near an array of antique farm implements, in front of a handsome new half-timbered barn that matches the nearby house. As Chuck and I arrived, Jim and Elaine emerged to greet us, offering a tour of the premises.

With proceeds from the sale of their California properties, they had purchased a three-thousand-square-foot mock-Tudor home surrounded by three acres of pasture and woods. A short drive from the center of an attractive town, the house and outbuildings perched on a hillside overlooking a lush river valley. Inside, the bedrooms, offices, living spaces, stairways, and landings were deeply carpeted. A cream-colored wood stove heated the high-ceilinged great room; fireplaces graced the music room and the master bedroom suite.

In the attached garage, beside tidy ranks of electrical control panels and battery arrays, sat an elegant new convertible-top horse-drawn carriage, ready to hitch to a draft horse that the couple planned to acquire. A wood-burning cook stove awaited installment in the summer kitchen they were building, adjacent to the conventional indoor kitchen. Attic storage held a year's worth of inventoried provisions in sealed food-grade plastic buckets, along with cartons of new underwear, socks, toilet paper, and other domestic supplies likely to be unobtainable when—as Elaine put it—"the trucks stop rolling."

Jim had installed photovoltaic and solar hot-water panels on the roof and erected a residential-scale wind turbine atop a thirty-five-foot pole in the front yard. When he and Elaine had first arrived, they had planted a small orchard of fruit trees: numerous varieties, each in duplicate. With help from visiting interns, they fenced the sloping front pasture and constructed a daytime shelter there for two handsome brown-and-black nanny goats, who kept the household, Jim told us, "awash" in dairy products. He milked at nine o'clock in the morning and nine at night and could barely stay on top of the yield; he made cheese daily and shared the overflow with neighbors. He had recently acquired an old-fashioned Sears, Roebuck butter churn, which he was repairing and learning to use.

Jim had constructed the twenty-four-by-thirty-six-foot barn from a kit. It featured livestock stalls, hay storage, a milking stall, and a tack room on the ground floor, living quarters above. The barn roof supported a rainwater catchment setup for the garden, supplying two 2500-gallon tanks tucked into the woods. A high-flow, 110-foot well backed up the city drinking water. Seeds were stored in a temperature-controlled space; greenhouses held seedlings; a hydroponic system for raising edible fish was in the works.

The homestead looked enviably self-sufficient. Not only did it provide abundantly for shelter, warmth, water, power, food; it was also beautifully situated, inviting, serene. But although the property was paid off and neither Jim nor Elaine needed to earn a salary, the couple could hardly find a moment to enjoy their handiwork. Hurrying from coop to garden to storage room, Elaine enumerated tasks that had yet to be accomplished. When Chuck and I admired the music room—its piano and sheet music set beside an overstuffed couch, its string and percussion instruments and stacks of CDs—she bemoaned the lack of time to use it. Someday soon, Jim said, they hoped to initiate a weekly music night.

They invited us to relax for a while, excusing themselves to finish up some chores. While Chuck explored the grounds, I investigated the extensive library, where titles leapt urgently from book spines: *Collapse; Extinction; The Coming Dark Age; The Long Emergency; The Party's Over; When Technology Fails; Friendly Fascism: A Grim Forecast of a Possible Totalitarian Future.* Browsing the collection, I felt increasingly ill at ease. As a longtime observer of mounting global crises brought on by human greed, ignorance, and overpopulation, I found few surprises on Jim and Elaine's shelves. To encounter such frank treatment of these urgent matters with which I was all too familiar should, I thought, have energized me. Instead, I was blindsided by a wave of dread.

It struck me that Jim and Elaine were facing this juncture in history with uncommon clarity. For them, it was an emergency. Notwithstanding the widespread apathy surrounding them, they insisted on living as if the world were plunging headlong into disaster. Many of my own day-to-day actions, in contrast, failed to reflect my supposed awareness. At the moment, my choices seem to suggest, there's still potable water in the pipes (though it sometimes smells terrible) and affordable gasoline at the pump (never mind how its use ravages the air, the water, the earth, and the climate). In my little corner of the world, there's plenty of nutritious food to eat. If you watched me go about my business, you might infer that I had no idea how inequitable and precarious it all is.

For Jim and Elaine, denial has become an unaffordable luxury—one that impending events will soon render obsolete. Even middle-class Americans who have so far avoided serious material deprivation or social breakdown may, in the not-too-distant future, face such difficulties—joining the billions of global citizens who have long known what it means to lack fresh drinking water, nutritious meals, affordable health care, secure housing or safe neighborhoods. Not only long-term sustainability but also immediate survival may depend on all-out efforts now. *High time to get ready*, shouted the library books, while Jim and Elaine's example pointed up the extent of my own denial.

When the four of us came together for a meal, Jim and Elaine held forth on their project and their vision. They talked of withdrawing in every way possible from what they called "the culture," which they considered hopelessly co-opted by a profit-driven system of economic greed, political corruption, military aggression, and corporate control. They made frequent references to the September 2001 attacks, which they assumed had been not just enabled but engineered by the Bush-Cheney administration. Anybody who thought otherwise, said Jim, was either ignoring the evidence or lost in wishful thinking.

I wasn't so sure. I could see that there would be clear benefits for the administration in Washington of disguising a homegrown bloodbath as an attack by foreign terrorists. The September 11 attacks sowed fear and passivity across the land, clearing the way for a profound erosion of domestic civil liberties. It provided an excuse for military adventures in oil-rich lands and lined the pockets of corporate war profiteers. I did recognize that the official 9/11 story contained blank spots and inconsistencies. At best, the Bush White House had ignored clear and specific warnings from its own intelligence gatherers, perhaps deliberately choosing to leave the country vulnerable to a major terrorist attack. Still, I couldn't accept our friends' grim certainty that U.S. hands had actively toppled the Twin Towers.

Jim and Elaine were also convinced that the United States had seen its last election, that the current regime—with the aid of another strategically timed "terrorist" catastrophe before November 2008—planned to install itself indefinitely in the White House. They seemed to assume that Chuck and I shared these views. I'd heard such arguments before; I found them horrifyingly plausible, if not thoroughly convincing.

Jim brought up the subject of radio-frequency identification (RFID) chips. These small electronic devices were being placed in livestock animals, he told us, ostensibly as a means of tracing pathogens to their sources during outbreaks of mad cow, bird flu, and other animal-borne diseases. But Elaine pointed out that where this technology was required as part of livestock registration systems, it was being imposed only on smaller farmers. Those individuals were required to pay for the chips' installation and monitoring, while giant corporate feedlot operations, she told us, were exempt.

The deeper goal behind RFID, she and Jim argued, was threefold: to make a handy profit for the corporations that own the technology, to further burden already marginalized independent farmers, and to accustom the rest of us to the idea that someday soon we would all be required to carry around the electronic brands—in our wallets or implanted under our skin.

"I've heard about this," I said, "in my volunteer work with the American Civil Liberties Union. The ACLU has been working to prevent governments and businesses from perpetrating civil liberties abuses with RFID chips." Elaine and Jim nodded and changed the subject. I knew that as far as they were concerned, the apathetic American citizenry had become terminally complicit in the erosion of our constitutional rights. And now they seemed uninterested in the work of those activists across the country who have never given up fighting for justice. As far as Jim and Elaine were concerned, apparently, those efforts were laughably ineffectual in the face of the fascist force bearing down on us all.

As we lingered at the table, my neck and shoulders grew knotted and stiff, and acid trickled in my gut. I felt as if I had shrunk by several inches. I stretched and took a few deep breaths—and tears began to leak from my eyes.

"Are you all right?" asked Elaine.

"Sure," I replied shakily. "It's just that all of this brings up a lot of, I guess, fear and grief." Jim, washing dishes at the kitchen sink, glanced over at me. "*What* does?" he asked.

"You know . . . ," I murmured, searching for what troubled me so acutely, "encroaching apocalypse?" Jim turned silently back to his task, apparently uncomfortable with the emotion in my voice. Elaine put away the last of the food and suggested we tour the garden.

Later, I voiced a question that had been nagging at me. "When times get tough, you two will be better equipped to thrive than most of your neighbors—than almost everybody around here. How do you imagine you'll respond if desperate, hungry people come up your driveway? I mean, it's not like you're some backwoods survivalists holed up with stockpiles of weapons. . . . "

"We do have guns," Elaine interjected quietly, "and we're learning how to use them."

"And practicing with the archery equipment, too," added Jim. "Of course, that's mainly for hunting. For the most part, we don't think we'll be a conspicuous target."

Elaine hastened to add that she planned to prepare a supply of small "care packages" to distribute to those who might come seeking handouts—more a token of sympathy and solidarity, she admitted, than a solution. "We feel it's important to be able to 'put on our own oxygen masks' first," she said. "Otherwise, there's no chance of helping anyone else."

Yet others didn't seem to want their help. One new intern departed for home within a day of arriving. She was young and innocent, said Elaine, and unwilling to face the truths on offer at the lifeboat training school. In spite of their civic activities, Elaine continued, she and Jim were finding it difficult to make local friends. Few of their townspeople, especially families with children, seemed eager to entertain the notion of imminent crisis, let alone to prepare for it.

"It's lonely enough when others say, 'I admire what you're doing, even though I'm not there,'" she said. "But most people don't even want to *look* at what we're doing. They think we're totally strange."

After a brief tour of the nearby town, Chuck and I took our leave. Driving south through gray, wet weather, I contemplated the rear of the car in front of us, its Oregon plate sporting a lone majestic conifer. I looked around at the hills rising above the highway. Over the past century or so, these woods had been transformed from verdant cathedrals into spindly plantations. They were patchworked with miles of muddy shaved rectangles, ugly with fallen snags and uprooted stumps. Ninety-nine percent of the range's old-growth forest had been clear-cut. Here and there, for reasons beyond our ken, loggers had left a few forlorn giants standing atop high ridges, where they remained silhouetted conspicuously against the horizon—ragged, unprotected, waiting to topple in the next stiff wind.

2. In the Stormy Dark

A few months later, I returned to the Northwest—this time for a two-month art and writing residency on a wildly beautiful headland clothed in native grasses and mossy old-growth woods. The program was small; when the staff commuted home in the evenings, I shared the premises with only three other artists. From the outset, all of us were intent on using our precious time at the art center as productively as we could. We enjoyed brief conversations at the mail drop and took occasional walks together on local trails; once in a while, we shared meals at each other's kitchen tables. Mostly, though, we kept to ourselves. Reveling in the freedom to shape my solitary days as I pleased, I dove deep into work while hours passed uncounted. I ate and slept according to the dictates of appetite and need. Most evenings, I called Chuck in California to share affection and news.

Those rhythms shifted when big weather arrived. In early December, storms of uncommon ferocity hammered the region with ninety-mile-an-hour winds and torrential blasts of rain and hail. Screaming gusts tore limbs off the spruces and Douglas-firs that surrounded my little cabin, hurling them to the roof with crashes and thuds. On the first night of gale-force bluster, I eyed the skylight directly above the mattress in my sleeping loft and carried my bedding down the ladder to make up the daybed downstairs.

Roads flooded; big trees fell helter-skelter. Power and phone lines crashed for miles up and down the coast, with utility companies predicting that repairs might take several days. Businesses in nearby communities shut down. With the electric heater off, I had to spend a chunk of each day stoking the fire and stocking my personal woodpile—fetching armloads of soggy split logs from an open shed and setting them inside to dry. Unable to use the electric kitchen appliances, I kept a pot of hot water and another of beans on two burner-sized rounds atop the woodstove.

I worked at my laptop computer until the battery died, then wrote in longhand by candlelight and D-cell-powered lantern. Having been told that a stilled electric pump might cause the local water supply to fail, I kept a couple of buckets full to the brim.

The power outage served up a vivid reminder: my daily life, even at its simplest, depends on energy and supplies whose sources lie beyond my personal control. For me, this particular experience of deprivation was merely a temporary adventure; it would last less than a week, with crews working day and night to open roads and restore power. I had enough batteries and canned food to ride out the storm. Nevertheless, I was acutely aware that if electricity were to become indefinitely unavailable or unaffordable—if the water main or my sources of basic supplies ran dry—then my compatriots and I would be up a mighty big creek.

It was a brief, rain-soaked preview of post–Peak Oil woes and an edifying sequel to the visit at Jim and Elaine's. Little about the experience truly surprised me—with one exception. I didn't mind eating canned chili or working by lantern light, and I enjoyed the necessary ritual of feeding a fire. Yet as the storm time deepened, one discomfort became unexpectedly acute: my need for human company. With phones out of commission, I couldn't carry on conversations with Chuck—my long-distance source of reliable companionship. I couldn't quite admit that I felt lonely or afraid; suddenly, though, the creative solitude that I had been relishing lost its savor. I wanted to be with other members of my tribe.

And so, it turned out, did my fellow residents. One stormy night, we went looking for each other. We all ended up together in the largest of the center's apartments—lighting candles, pooling odd assortments of food from our rapidly warming refrigerators, making stone soup on the woodstove.

I brought a guitar. We wrapped ourselves in blankets, drank wine, laughed, shared artwork and songs, ate chocolate and tangerines. As nourished by communion as by the feast, I recalled the refrain from "Telling Stories" by songwriter Greg Brown. Every one of us, Brown points out, is frightened and alone. When dark times befall us, what our spirits need most is the company of others, telling stories around the fire.

I told my fellow refugees about my previous summer's visit to Jim and Elaine's place. I admitted that I still felt disturbed by my experience there—that I was trying to comprehend the panicky dread that lingered in my gut.

In response, someone shared a story about a man who had built an off-the-grid fortress in the wake of the Cuban missile crisis in the early 1960s. Anticipating nuclear holocaust, he used his considerable means to purchase a remote piece of property in rural Oregon, inhabiting it with a small group of comrades. Thick steel panels slid over the windows of his large main house; multiple barns stored years' worth of provisions, and an underground tank held ten thousand gallons of propane fuel. My companion didn't know much more about the man and his walled compound—only that, eventually, he changed his mind, put his property on the market, and applied to rabbinical school.

At about nine o'clock that night, there was a flicker and a hum, and the electricity came back on. We let out a collective whoop of joy. The light's return seemed all the sweeter for being shared.

3. Leaning into the Light

Long after I had returned home to California, the brief sojourn at Jim and Elaine's place continued to reverberate in my mind and emotions. I'd certainly received a useful wake-up call: a challenge to my habitual denial, a reminder about the tenuousness of the comforts of life as I know it, an exhortation to respond to the true emergency of these times. But my discomfort went even deeper than this. Despite much that I found admirable in the lifeboat enterprise, something about it did not sit right with me, and I needed to understand why.

I told the story to many people and witnessed a range of reactions. Some friends shared Jim and Elaine's sense of urgency and admired the couple's proactive pursuits, while others dismissed them as paranoid nuts. Some decried what they perceived as political myopia and unconscious privilege on Jim and Elaine's part. Still others observed that while the lifeboat appeared in some ways to be a sane response to dangerous times, the project also seemed mired in lonely, self-defeating fear. In each response, I found a kernel of truth. Collectively, these rattled around in my ethical kaleidoscope; I shifted the lens this way and that, holding it to the light, looking for a pattern.

The criticism that Jim and Elaine might be blind to their own socioeconomic privilege struck me as important. In a local news story about the lifeboat project, the couple asserted that "if *we* can create a self-sufficient life, then anybody can." To make such a claim was to discount the money, time, and expertise their efforts required—resources that lie beyond most people's reach. They rarely acknowledged the billions around the world who are already intimate with economic and environmental apocalypse—as if the plight of those desperate and disenfranchised people (and other beings) were unconnected to the fears of middle-class Americans.

In characterizing their project as an experiment in self-sufficiency, Jim and Elaine were ignoring the extent to which their haven of self-reliance rested on a history of labor, materials, and ecosystems not of their own making. Their endeavors called into question the limits of individual self-sufficiency. While it's prudent to accomplish what we can at the household level, the world's people can't build a few billion lifeboats; there aren't enough resources to go around.

Nor did I find it especially helpful to think in terms of "completely withdrawing from the culture," as Jim and Elaine put it. Contemporary culture as we know it may be dominated by rapacious transnational corporations, military powers, media monopolies, and antidemocratic forces—but it also includes every public library and farm-to-school initiative, every citizen antigang youth-empowerment program and listener-sponsored public radio station, every alternative-energy project, every piece of inspiring literature to be found on the lifeboat's shelves. To react to repression and greed by turning our backs on "the culture"—that is, on the collective expressions of a diverse and multilayered society—means to tune out the instruments of our potential liberation.

Jim and Elaine equated hopefulness about such possibilities with wishful thinking, decrying hope as a naive, self-defeating emotion. But hope can also be a compass that guides us toward the light. "If you assume that there's no hope, you guarantee that there will be no hope," wrote critic Noam Chomsky. "If you assume that there is an instinct for freedom, that there are opportunities to change things, there's a chance you may contribute to making a better world."

If every U.S. citizen had assumed, as Jim and Elaine did, that the 2008 elections were lost before they began, then that prophecy might have fulfilled itself. Of course, turning the planetary ship around demands a level of social transformation far more profound than a change of personnel in Washington, as events since January 2009 have amply demonstrated. But how can we ever achieve the necessary shift in consciousness and action—a Great Turning, as Joanna Macy and other spiritual, political, and environmental visionaries have called it—if we cease to believe in the capacity of our fellow humans for good, in the significance of every small triumph and every light-giving act along the way? How can we learn to survive future deprivations if we can't feel gratitude for the gifts we are blessed with right now? How can we make a world we want our grandchildren to live in if we expect to kill each other in the process?

For that expectation seemed implicit in the lifeboat's charted course. Jim and Elaine had weapons, they explained, not only because they might someday need to defend themselves against armed gangs but also because they believed citizen nonviolence under a violent state is a dangerous, deluded stance. They recommended Ward Churchill's *Pacifism as Pathology*, which questions the efficacy of historical nonviolent movements from Gandhi to MLK. Churchill argues that pacifists' desire to be "good and nice people" (to quote the book's preface by Derrick Jensen) may actually undermine progressive social change.

Churchill and others challenge, sometimes in compelling ways, the assumption that nonviolence is always the morally preferable choice. They point out that pacifist responses to terrorism and tyranny can backfire, enabling rather than quelling violence. Nevertheless, absent certainty about when, if ever, homicide might be justifiable, I choose to err on the side of nonviolence. I don't want to spend my limited time and energy preparing to kill my neighbors. I may find myself one day facing the barrel of a gun and regretting my choice—but I remain troubled by Jim and Elaine's righteous certainty about theirs.

I guess it's that righteous air that bothered me most. Jim and Elaine did a lot more talking than listening. When they spoke of donning oxygen masks in order to rescue others, they projected an image of themselves as capable grownups overseeing helpless children. When we corresponded after the visit, Elaine informed me that she and Jim had hoped in vain that my tears at their breakfast table had indicated a true "awakening"—as if I were a benighted soul they had expected to enlighten.

Jim and Elaine claimed a stance of muscular political realism: "tough love" in a dangerous world. It's not a form of love I respond to. A degree of humility and openness would have engaged me more readily. For those of us who want to work with each other toward short-term human survival as well as the planet's long-term sustainability, I believe attitude matters. Nobody has the one true secret to success. As Barry Lopez put it, "There are simply no answers to some of the great pressing questions. You continue to live them out, making your life a worthy expression of a leaning into the light."

If I were a quicker, bolder interlocutor, I might have articulated these criticisms in the course of my conversations with Jim and Elaine around their kitchen table. I might have heard their responses and contributed to a productive exchange. Instead, I listened in mute unease, and in the years since, I've been groping my way toward insight. As I struggle to understand the sinking feeling I experienced aboard the lifeboat, I keep recalling one particular exchange that took place toward the end of our visit. Over breakfast, Chuck mentioned that he was training as a hospice volunteer, to serve people in our community during their last months of life. Jim responded with genuine puzzlement: "That's a noble sentiment. But why choose that path in this urgent time? Why would an intelligent person like you, someone who understands the global crises we're facing, want to spend his limited time and energy at the bedsides of dying folks?"

I think Jim's question goes to the heart of my misgivings about Jim and Elaine's way of seeing. People who are dying or suffering—all of us, at some point—need succor and compassion, whether in stable times or in the midst of crisis. Jim seemed to presume that to face great, sweeping dangers requires us to stop taking care of each other, person to person. I feel quite the opposite. If we abandon each other as individuals, how can we save ourselves as a species? Those who ignore the everyday need for loving care are liable, it seems to me, to end up barricaded alone in a gun-filled fortress with steel windows, atop a giant tank of flammable fuel.

Sustainability entails more than catchment tanks and backyard chickens; it's a matter of the spirit. If we are to make the world a less frightening and more survivable place, then stockpiling supplies is no more urgent a task than nurturing compassion and interdependence. I find strength for the struggle in the kindness of those willing to tend the sick and the dying; in the contributions of activists and naturalists, farmers and teachers; in the sustenance that my fellow artists bring to the stone soup. When it's dark and cold outside, I want the company of others sitting around the fire telling stories. And while I treasure solitude and honor diligence, I crave companions who make raucous use of the music room—even before the solar panels are on the roof.

Acknowledgments

This collection emerged over the course of so many years that a few of the people who sharpened my ideas, reviewed drafts, or provided advice and encouragement may no longer remember doing so. Worse, I have inevitably omitted some essential names below. I extend gratitude to everyone whom I have failed to acknowledge explicitly. You know who you are—and I will awake in the middle of the night and remember.

For helping bring this book into being, I thank Elizabeth Abrams, Jenny and John Anderson, Carolyn Atkinson, Chuck Atkinson, Nathan and Julie Atkinson, Seth Atkinson, Barbara Bash, Jacquie Bellon, Jessica Bender, Eli Bernstein, Severin Borenstein, Frank and Jane Boyden, Melissa Braden, Zelda Bronstein, Scott Brookie, Martha Brown, Ginger Burley, John Calderazzo and SueEllen Campbell, Sarah Carvill, Kathy Chetkovich, Rita Clagett, Richard Connor, Deborah DeWit, Robin Drury, David James Duncan, Esther Ehrlich, Ellen Farmer, Farnaz Fatemi, Alisa Fineman, Tom Fleischner, Carol Freeman, Cissy Freeman, Greg Gilbert, Katy Gilmore, Steve Gliessman, Kaitlin Gregg, Elmer and Pam Grossman, Ed Grumbine, Conn Hallinan, Anne Hayes, Ava and Gernot Heinrichsdorff, Peg Herring, Hannah Hinchman, Tony Hiss, Annamieka Hopps, Carol Howard,

Parker Huber, Robbie Jaffe, Ken Kann, Jenny Keller, Alan Kesselheim, Nancy Krusoe, Jenny Kurzweil, Yael Lachman, Michael Lawrence, Tracye Lea Lawson, Leslie Lopez, Fran and Joanna Macy, Jacquelyn Marie, Joan Martens, Mary Kay Martin, Christian McEwen, Nancy Migdall, Doug Mosel, Joanne Mulcahy, Pat Musick, Gary Nabhan, Julia Nace, Ellen Newberry, Arlyn Osborne, Anna Paganelli, Larry Pageler, Ingrid Parker, Stephanie Pass, Juliet Peck, Daniel Press, Bob Pyle, Martha and Norman Rabkin, Irene Reti, Alan Richards, Don Rothman, Susan Sanford, Carol Savonen, Craig Schindler, Kirk Schroeder, Robert Shetterly, Paul Skenazy, Inguna Skuja, Roz Spafford, Kim Stafford, Anne Stine, Amber Coverdale Sumrall, Andie Thrams, Jude Todd, Susan Tweit, Breck Tyler, Patrice Vecchione, Jesse Virago, Phil Ward, Susan Watrous, Casey Watson, Amy Weaver, Ken Weisner, Robin White, John Wilkes, George Wuerthner, Erika Zavaleta, Ann Zwinger, and Susan Zwinger.

I received support and inspiration from Sitka Center for Art and Ecology, at Cascade Head, OR; the University of Washington's H. R. Whiteley Center, at Friday Harbor Labs; New Camaldoli Hermitage, in Big Sur, CA; Santa Sabina Center, in San Rafael, CA: the Professional Development Committee of UC-AFT Local 2199; the Littermates; the Salonistas; the WhooHas; David James Duncan's 2004 University of Montana Environmental Writing Institute; Amber Coverdale Sumrall's and Carolyn Foster's writing-and-spirit workshops; Joanna Macy's Summer 2006 Intensive in the Work That Reconnects; *Writing Nature* and the Crestone, CO, writers' gatherings, and the Writing Program, the Program in Community and Agroecology, and the Department of Environmental Studies at UC Santa Cruz.

Special thanks are due to Jenny Kurzweil and Christian McEwen for their essential feedback on manuscript drafts, to Sandy Bell for her beautiful cover design, and to Don Rothman for his artful photo. The remarkable Irene Reti of Juniper Lake Press saw this project through in more ways than I can count. Ellen Setteducati's meticulous copyediting made this a better book; any remaining errors result from my own carelessness or style choices.

I am profoundly grateful to Chuck Atkinson—poet, husband, reader, love of my life. I couldn't be in better hands.

ABOUT THE AUTHOR

Sarah Juniper Rabkin is an award-winning teacher of writing and environmental studies at the University of California, Santa Cruz. She grew up in Berkeley in the 1960s and 1970s and studied biology at Harvard and science communication at UC Santa Cruz. She has worked as a high school teacher, workshop leader, Q&A columnist, oral history interviewer, and freelance editor. As a volunteer activist, she has helped advocate for labor fairness, civil liberties, GLBT rights, and natural history education. Rabkin lives near the shore of Monterey Bay with her husband, poet Charles Atkinson.

Photo: Don Rothman

ABOUT JUNIPER LAKE PRESS

Juniper* Lake Press publishes fiction, creative nonfiction, and poetry, with an emphasis on feminist, lesbian, Jewish, and/or environmental literature. Located in Capitola, California, the press is run by Irene Reti, also proprietor of HerBooks Feminist Press from 1984 to 2001. For more information on Juniper Lake Press and the backlist of HerBooks titles, please see www.juniperlakepress.com.

---

*The congruence with Sarah Rabkin's middle name is purely coincidental.